INSIDE THE MIND OF A MUSICIAN

SU TERRY

Inside the Mind of a Musician

Copyright © 2016 by Su Terry
All Rights Reserved
ISBN: 978-0-9859245-7-7
Published by Qi Note

The content herein was previously published, with some alteration, under the title
Greatest Hits of the Blog That Ate Brooklyn:
Inside the Mind of a Musician

The poem "Just When You Thought" was previously published (under the pen name Susan Tatarsky) in Arbella Magazine.

ACKNOWLEDGEMENTS

Many thanks to my friends, relatives and colleagues who appear in these pages. Thanks also to the many anonymous passersby who contributed to this book with their mere presence.

I'm grateful to Gil Barretto for his love and support; Derwyn Holder for his perspective, Richard Frank for his jokes, and my assistant Sandy Payson for her indefatigability.

I'm indebted to my friend and Brooklyn neighbor, author Don Gabor. His advice and guidance gave me the reality check I needed–thanks Don!

ST

> Photos of Su by James Richard Kao
> Cover Design by Ana Grigoriu

Musicians are creatures of the absurd.

–Michael A. Coon

AUTHOR'S PREFACE

Have you ever wanted to get inside the mind of a musician? Step right up, folks! Here she is, a real live Baby Boomer Chick Jazz Musician from Brooklyn!

While perhaps not as interesting as that of the Strong Man or the Bearded Lady, life as a musician is only slightly to the right of surreal. And I guarantee there's no better place to observe the world than from the bandstand, where I have watched the antics of kings, paupers and middle class humanity on five continents for a few decades now (but only during the rests). The number one requirement for being in the music business? A highly developed sense of humor.

Writing has also been a lifelong love–wrote my first words when I was knee-high to a crayon. When I was in high school, Dad hired me to do his writing assignments for his job. He kicked back on the couch with WQXR FM cranked through the headphones while I slaved away in longhand. When it was time for college I went to music school, because my parents said I should keep up my jazz saxophone playing just in case the writing thing didn't work out.

Please note that while much of the material herein is timeless, some of it reflects the time period in which it was originally written–2005 to 2009.

I hope you enjoy reading these personal, comedic, tragic, and slightly eccentric paragraphs as much as I enjoyed writing them. I feel better now.

Su Terry
Brooklyn, New York

CONTENTS

ACKNOWLEDGMENTS

AUTHOR'S PREFACE

I'M NOT A ROCK STAR, BUT I PLAY ONE ON 'THE SIMS'   1

    I'M NOT A ROCK STAR, BUT I PLAY ONE ON 'THE SIMS'

    GEN-AD

    THE SAME OLD STORY

    TV STAR NON-SIGHTING

    PLAN B

    OLYMPIC TV

    I'M CONFESSIN'

    IS GOD INTERESTED?

    I KID YOU NOT

    WHERE ARE THE HEROES

    HILLARY CLINTON CAMPAIGN SONG

    FILMING

    SIX MILLION

    CHIMPS VS KIDS

    JODIE FOSTER

    PLAYING PUNDIT

    TIMING IS EVERYTHING

ON THE ROAD AGAIN   20

ON THE ROAD AGAIN
THE PRINCIPAL IS YOUR PAL?

DRIVING DIRECTIONS

EAU CLAIRE, WI

MY ANCESTRY

PULLED OVER FOR AN AUTOGRAPH

ROAD RAGE

THE FIRST TIME I SET FOOT IN ENGLAND

HOLY DAZE, BATMAN

ANTI-LOCK BRAKE SYSTEM

CAR RENTAL

LONDON CALLING

REVENGE AT LAST!

WTF

GAS

TSA=GOD

TORONTO IAJE

X DRIVING SCHOOL

SHOCK, DENIAL, ANGER, ACCEPTANCE

EFFICIENCY, I LOVE IT

ELEUTHRA

OSAMA HATES JAZZ 40

OSAMA HATES JAZZ

CALL FOR MUSICIANS

TONIGHT'S GIG

ELEVATOR MUSIC

FAKE KING COLE

BARRY'S BDAY

EVERYTHING IS RELATIVE

JAM SESSION ETIQUETTE

AND ANOTHER THING

SAVING THE BEST FOR LAST

ONCE MORE, WITH FEELING

TOP GUN

I'LL HAVE TO GO WITH DESTINY ON THIS ONE

COOL VS DORK

FEINSTEIN'S

THESE ARE THE GOOD TIMES

SITTING IN

HAROLD VICK

MY OWN STUFF

MY LATEST IMPROVISATION

COUNTRY MUSIC DOES NOT NECESSARILY SUCK

TRUMPET PLAYERS

JVC JAZZ PARTY

ELLINGTON & STRAYHORN

JAM SESSION PROTOCOL

CARING FOR THE NOTES

DIGGING THE ZEITGEIST   64

DIGGING THE ZEITGEST

AS THE RATWHEEL TURNS

ON THE TOWN

HUMOR, THE 7TH SENSE

RATWHEEL RULES

WHAT'S THE POINT

GAME OF LIFE

OBJETS DE MUSIQUE: IDENTITY CHIPS W/ DIP

CELLPHONES ARE THE NEW CIGARETTES

SCHUMANN RESONANCE

JUST WONDERING

PUBLIC SERVICE ANNOUNCEMENT

TRIBES, ETC.

DATED, SHMATED

STILL THE SAME OLD STORY

THE END OF CHRISTMAS

THE NEW YEAR'S GIG

SO, YOU WANT TO BE MY "MYSPACE FRIEND"

MUSIC-AN AURAL TRADITION

SORRY, WE'RE CLOSED

IF CONSTRUCTION SITES WERE BROADWAY SHOWS

ZEITGEIST, REDUX

BROOKLYN SERENADE   86

BROOKLYN SERENADE

NEGOTIATING

    TO KILL A MOCKINGBIRD

    IT'S MY BLOG AND I'LL BITCH IF I WANT TO

    STRIKE UPDATE

    THE VIEW FROM BERNSTEIN'S GRAVE

    EPISODE 23

    I THINK I MIGHT BE IN THE WRONG LIFE

    THE CUSTOMER IS ALWAYS WRONG

    FUN WITH MYSPACE

    GRAND PRIZE

    NYC MARATHON

    LIVE STRONG-EAT YOUR VEGETABLES

    THE COST OF DOING BUSINESS

    A "MARTHA" DAY

    SUMMER IN THE CITY

    ROBERT'S BIKE TRIP

    HAUNTED APARTMENT?

    BEN FRANKLIN'S LEGACY

    SUPER PLUMBER

    MY ANNUAL DAY AT THE BEACH

THE EAGLE FLIES ON FRIDAY   108

    THE EAGLE FLIES ON FRIDAY

    PENSION PACKAGE PERKS

    CECI N'EST PAS UNE CHECK

    GRAMMY AWARDS

HELLO, YOU'RE SUPPOSED TO GET PAID FOR THIS

JACKIE O

THE END OF PROFESSIONAL MUSICIANS, 2ND INSTALLMENT

HOW TO MILK A PER DIEM

ANYONE WANT TO BUY A BRIDGE?

UPDATE ON PHOTO SCENARIO

WHO LIKES WHOM?

YOU WON! NOW GIVE US YOUR SONG FOR FREE

STILL THE SAME OLD BIZ

INSURANCE UPDATE

YOU CAN'T AUTOGRAPH A DOWNLOAD

JAZZ BIZ

WHOSE LAW

TOUGH BUSINESS

OIL, OR LACK THEREOF

THE LYRICS OF LIFE   129

THE LYRICS OF LIFE

DRUGS

PURPOSE IN LIFE

A JOURNEY TO INFINITY BEGINS WITH A SINGLE STEP

LONELINESS

LAWRENCE FERLINGHETTI

SECRETS

"SHEESH"

I ONLY USE MY POWERS FOR GOOD

CARS OF THE STARS

SERIOUSLY-THE JOKE IS DEAD

PAM'S PARTY

HACKING THE DICTIONARY

JUST WHEN YOU THOUGHT

BACK TO SERIOUS STUFF

GRANDMA & GRANDPA

HALLOWEEN & COSTUMES

RIFFING ON A SUNDAY AFTERNOON HAIKU

HAIR SALON 101

MARCH TOWARD MATRIARCHY? START WITH THE LADIES ROOM

THE SICKENING QUOTIDITY OF REALITY

SURGEON GENERAL SPEAKS

WHEN HARRY MET ZSA ZSA . . .

PAULO COELHO

A HALF CENTURY OF MAGAZINE SUBSCRIPTIONS

SUNDAY TIMES TIDBITS

A NEW POEM

REFLECTIONS ON TRAVIS

WILD TURKEY COURTSHIP RITUAL

CREDO

ENGLISH

OK, POETRY LOVERS . . .

21ST CENTURY AMERICAN KOAN

TECH DIFFICULTIES, PLEASE STAND BY   157

TECH DIFFICULTIES, PLEASE STAND BY
SOLSTICE
EQUINOX
A RIDE BY ANY OTHER NAME

RETRACTION

BAKING BREAD

IT AIN'T EASY BEING A FILL IN THE BLANK

GENDER MISIDENTIFICATION

WHEN THEY SAY 'CONTROL TOP' THEY AIN'T KIDDIN'

FISH STORY

HEY-DON'T TOUCH THE ANTENNAE

MY LIFE IS GREAT, HOW 'BOUT YOURS?

SECRET CODE

COMPUTER CAPER GONE WRONG

CECIL PAYNE

DRESSING ROOMS, OR LACK THEREOF

REPLACE CAPACITOR ON CIRCUIT BOARD, PIECE OF CAKE

GIGABYTES?

TRANSPOSING: TRY IT AT HOME FIRST

HERE I GO AGAIN

NOT THE JET PACK OF MY DREAMS

YOU & YOUR IPOD

REEDS

SUBWAY COMPLAINTS

MUSIC RULES

STUDENT AWARD

ABOUT THE AUTHOR

BY THE SAME AUTHOR

INDEX

READER DISCUSSION GUIDE

Inside the Mind of a Musician

I'M NOT A ROCK STAR BUT I PLAY ONE ON "THE SIMS"

Terry

I'M NOT A ROCK STAR BUT I PLAY ONE ON "THE SIMS"

I've always loved the sound of church bells. Whenever I hear them, they capture my attention. They seem symbolic of ages long past, connecting us to days of yore with their expressive vibrations.

In some towns you visit or drive through, the church steeples are still the highest buildings. It's even like that in certain sections of Brooklyn, like on 4th Avenue near my apartment.

The churches in my neighborhood are Polish. As you can imagine, in my neighborhood we also have plenty of stuffed cabbage and kielbasa.

One time, when I first moved to this neighborhood, I grabbed a hunk of kielbasa from the fridge to munch on while waiting for the subway—a little protein to start the day. Keep in mind that the subway stations in the outer reaches of New York City are a far cry from the streamlined transportation hubs in Midtown, festooned with mosaics and decorative tile. Rather, 25th Street Station's grim, dank walls and dirty tile (not to mention the occasional rodent—and I don't mean Mickey) are reminiscent of some war-torn Bolshevik terminus.

So as I ate my chunk of kielbasa in the 25th Street subway station, it suddenly hit me: I'm in Eastern Europe. It's Warsaw,1952, and I'm on my way to the headquarters of the underground newspaper with a shoulder bag full of samizdat that I just smuggled across the border.

Inside the Mind of a Musician

This fantasy reminds me of a real-life adventure in East Berlin in 1988, where I hung out with some authentic underground activists and was followed by the secret police.

Have I ever told you that story?

The other day I mentioned this to Don Gabor, who said, "My dear, EVERYONE in East Berlin in 1988 was followed by the secret police."

But I digress. Back to the church bells:

Yesterday I played a gig at a Catholic school that was connected to a church, and as I was walking to the parking lot afterwards I heard the church bells ringing. But something about them seemed strange. As I got closer, I realized that the bells were ringing to the accompaniment of the electronic hum of an improperly grounded outlet, or—perhaps—yes—a very bad PA system.

Upon closer auditory inspection, the bells further revealed themselves to be tinny and depthless, clinching the utterly dismal realization that these were not church bells, but merely a recording of church bells.

The sounds emanating from this church spire, rather than evoking a connection to eons past and a hint of the existence of Higher Powers, instead trumpeted out with all the fidelity of sloganeering Nazis blaring over a loudspeaker in Dachau in 1944.

It seemed a perfect encapsulation of modern society —let's fire the bell guy and throw on a tape. Hey, we can even save money by putting it on a timer so the janitor won't have to turn it on twice a day!

Who needs real life when you can just watch it on TV?

Terry

GEN-AD

Why waste your money on regular advertising when you can have GEN-AD. We imprint your customized product information directly onto the DNA of your potential customers. No more fussing with print ads and TV–our advertising goes right to the core–literally!

Our advertising campaign for YOUR PRODUCT is not just for today's public, but for the next generation. Talk about thinking ahead!

No more "mama dadda." Baby's first words will be YOUR PRODUCT!

The Mummy wakes up after a thousand-year nap: the first thing he wants is not tanna leaves, but YOUR PRODUCT!

If people walked a mile for a Camel, now they'll skip a generation for YOUR PRODUCT!

Call today for pricing!

THE SAME OLD STORY

After my nephew's birthday party today, he and his friends were watching a cartoon where the characters were puppets. My sister-in-law Anna said it's called "American Team." There were these puppets in Middle Eastern garb speaking Arabic. One of them had a 'suspicious' looking briefcase.

I thought "Oh, this is going to be a twist, where these guys turn out to be in a band, or delivering bagels or something." But then they pulled out machine guns and started shooting everyone in this little outdoor plaza in Paris. Then the American Team came in a helicopter and blasted them away.

Okay, so the American Team took down the Eiffel Tower and blew up the Louvre in the process–but hey, they saved the good people of France! The stereotypes were really over the top. It was like the old movies and TV shows where all Germans were stupid, or all Japanese were evil, or all women were housewives or all black people were servants. Yes Virginia, history really does repeat itself. *Ad nauseam.*

TV STAR NON-SIGHTING

At my job last night in New Jersey with Rich Szabo's 9 piece band, he said that the three stars of Queer Eye for the Straight Guy were there. But since I have never seen the show, I don't know which ones they were. It's always like that, I never know anything about the current TV shows. (But I could tell you the plot of every episode of I Love Lucy and The Honeymooners.) When I was on the Sopranos last year, shooting a band scene, my friends asked me which of the stars were there, but I didn't know because I don't know what they look like. My neighbors Pat and Roger freaked when they saw my name in the credits. I went over and watched it with them on replay; "that's me, on the end– no, wait, hit rewind!"

PLAN B

My friend B., the radio announcer, had his show moved to another time slot because of a shake up at the studio. It seems that the Program Director wanted to give another announcer the old heave-ho, for reasons of quality control: it seems his show sucked.

Unfortunately for the Program Director, the announcer in question then threatened to kill himself. But

Terry

while the Program Director was looking up the number of the Suicide Hotline people, said announcer evidently came up with another plan. It seems that one of the station patrons, whose endowment is in the 8 million dollar range, is a listener of the show in question; indeed, it is the only show he listens to.

Some phone calls were exchanged. Through a Divine Act of Providence, the 'dollars ex machina' descended from above, and the man's show was reinstated, in a new and improved time slot, moreover.

My friend B. looks at it all with equanimity. He's also trolling all the County Clerk records within range of the station, for properties that point to Jazz Lovers of Distinction. Like they say, "a distinction a day keeps extinction away."

OLYMPIC TV

The NY Times reports that both "American Idol" and "Grey's Anatomy" (neither of which I've ever seen; but just like the critics, that doesn't stop me from commenting on them) beat the pants off the now-dressed (as opposed to formerly naked) Olympic events on television.

What does this prove? It proves that TV viewers, instead of watching people actually DO something superbly (i.e. athletes), would rather:

A. Watch people do something badly (i.e. most American Idol contestants)

B. Watch people pretend to do things (i.e. actors).

And I think that just about sums it up for the road ahead. Oh, and a side note: what about bringing back naked Olympics? Maybe just for the summer games...

Inside the Mind of a Musician

I'M CONFESSIN'

Apropos of my previous post titled "COUNTRY MUSIC DOES NOT NECESSARILY SUCK", I have another dirty little secret that's been weighing me down. I want, at this time, to make a public admission–I've got to get this out in the open.

You see, everyone thinks I'm so hip and cool–but being the torch-carrying Arbiter of Good Taste is such a responsibility. I mean, what would people say if they knew the truth?

Here it is:

Sometimes, I . . . listen to . . . (swallow). . . Lite FM.

I was listening to it in my car the other day. (I would never listen to it in my house–I have not yet reached that nadir of decadence.) And yes, I was alone.

The thing is, sometimes they play a really great song! "If You Leave Me Now", by Chicago! Killer song and arrangement, dude.

Problem: After turning on, tuning in and dropping out (of the 00's), and getting high off this 70's drug that is evidently still on the streets, YOU WANT MORE! One song is never enough! You keep listening, hoping that the next song, then the next, and the next, will be as good as the first. But it never is.

I realize I'm not hurting anyone but myself. But I can't stop.

IS GOD INTERESTED?

Heh heh, really sucked you in with the title of this entry, didn't I?

Today's entry is prompted by the DVD that Liz gave me, called "The Secret." It's all about the Law of Attraction,

Terry

which basically says that whatever you focus on with your feelings and your thoughts, you will attract to yourself.

So, here's today's rumination: Let's look at the universe from a Taoist point of view. This shows us an impartial universe that has no interest in human affairs, and recognizes only Energy as its operating principle.

Now let's take the seemingly opposite point of view: that one can pray to a God that will intervene in human affairs and possibly create a favorable outcome to a situation.

How does one reconcile these two views? Taking the assumption that we live in an impartial universe that operates only according to currents of energies, how would one pray for a favorable outcome to a situation, knowing that the universe couldn't care less?

When we realize that the Law of Attraction is not emotionally-based, but rather energy-based, we have the answer. When one prays, one sends a current of energy representing one's desire out into the universe. The universe merely responds to this current of energy with a like current, thus enabling the manifestation of one's prayer on the physical plane.

Are you still with me?

Do I sound too much like Tori Amos right now?

Anyway, I think I have very neatly solved this philosophical problem which has been troubling humankind since time immemorial.

No need to thank me.

In the words of Phil Woods, whom I saw today at the Yamaha Artist reception: "Pray for us, Zoot!"

This is only funny if you're a jazz musician, so I beg the indulgence of all other readers. Look, just to even things out, how about a little joke for all you scientists out there–

Inside the Mind of a Musician

True story: I gave Gil a couple of pieces of liver to distribute to the dogs. After half an hour he's still giving them pieces of liver! So I said, "What are you dividing that into–Planck's Constant?"

If you're a physicist, that should be a real knee-slapper.

I KID YOU NOT

I recently met a woman from the city of New Orleans, who assured me that in her native land the colloquial lingo for the plural of "pants" is "pantseses." Likewise, the plural of "breasts" is "breasteses." I kid you not.

Well, I guess it's because pants are already plural, so if you're talking about a bunch of pairs of pants, or breasts, certainly one would want to make that perfectly clear.

Wouldn't one?

And with the title of this post, I tip my chapeau to the venerable Jack Paar, host of the Tonight Show before Johnny Carson, who was before Jay Leno. "I kid you not" was his catch phrase. He would've had a ball with the "pantseses" bit.

I have this great record (yes–vinyl) of Paar doing his show live in England. He tells a story about running into a young lady at a party in London and knowing that he was supposed to know who she was, but drawing a blank. So he fishes:

"So, how's your brother?' She says, "I don't have a brother."

"Oh, that's right. How's your, uh, father?"
"Oh, father's been dead for quite some time."
"I'm terribly sorry! How's your. . . sister?"

Terry

"She's fine."
Long pause.
"Still Queen."

WHERE ARE THE HEROES

When I was a kid in school, we read kid-versions of the Greeks myths. At age ten or so, this was my first exposure to those classic tales. The heroes of those myths—Theseus, Heracles (Hercules), Perseus et. al.—earned their stripes largely by being of service to others. Slaying villains who preyed on unwary travelers, ridding villages of monsters, that sort of thing.

Now, more modern heroes come to mind: Florence Nightingale, Martin Luther King or Mother Teresa. Like their ancient, mythic counterparts, they transcended human limitations by giving themselves to noble causes that loomed, immense, before the tiny individual.

In the fifties we began to experience our heroes on the silver screen. They were, literally, larger than life. We could pretend to be them sometimes, and maybe be better people for it. In the seventies I saw The Thin Man for the first time. I wanted to be like Nora Charles. She was cool. She was sophisticated. She was funny. Nick adored her. So when she ordered five martinis and told the waiter "just line them up right here," I went out and tried the same thing. Never made it to number three. Soon enough I realized that drinking like a fish was not necessarily part of the archetypal menu.

Archetypes don't have to be confined to the narrow roles that modern society favors, however. Hey, in the myths, you had men, you had women, you had guys who were half-goat, you had chicks who were half-fish. And it was cool.

Inside the Mind of a Musician

As adults, we can find heroes to inspire us by merely looking at history. But where are the heroes for the kids? That's probably why a lot of little kids say they want to be firefighters, because the heroism there is very obvious. Plus the cool red truck.

Heroes are not defined by by their weaknesses, but by their strengths. All those horn players trying to be like Charlie Parker by emulating the habits that HE HIMSELF detested would have been better off sequestering themselves in the practice shed.

Gil says we do a thing because of the emotional feeling we get from it. For example, if a man wants to be a truck driver, it's because he wants the FEELING OF SATISFACTION AND POWER he thinks he will get from driving a truck. Apply this idea to fill-in-the-blank. The emotional center is what drives us. It's good at driving, but lousy at obeying traffic signals. If we only did what the emotional center wants in every situation, we would be acting like three-year-olds all the time. (Instead of only sometimes.) Nevertheless, emotions are the driving force behind everything we do.

Heroes appeal to our emotional center, and make us better people because of it. There are an awful lot of people on this planet, and more every day. Are there proportionally more heroes, then?

If not, there need to be.

Face your fears. Help somebody. Be kind to animals. If you've read this far, you're already a hero.

But we can always do more.

Terry

HILLARY CLINTON CAMPAIGN SONG

I understand that Hillary's team is looking for a campaign song, and they are inviting her supporters to suggest one. On her website, there are ten songs listed, with the option to suggest a different song.

I went over my list of possible Su Terry originals that could be submitted. For some reason, my song "Marry a Good Man" jumped into my mind. The chorus goes: "Marry a good man, who's gonna treat you right, each and every day, and all thruuuuuuuuuu the night." Uh, maybe not.

Well, what about "Makin' All The Same Mistakes"– hmmm, I don't think so.

Or "One Last Chance"–no, no, a thousand times no.

I guess I am just not cut out for this campaign song business. My songs are too depressing!

Perhaps if I really knuckle down I could come up with some cheery anthem or other. Can you imagine how much free publicity you would get if your song were a Presidential Candidate's theme song?

Wait a minute–does McCain have one yet?

FILMING

I'm in the middle of producing my first film. It's a demo DVD for a jazz education company for whom I do consulting work.

We needed some scenes of New York and the jazz clubs, so the other night I drove a Jeep Grand Cherokee down Broadway while filmmaker John Halpern and his assistant Courtney were squeezed through the sunroof, each with a giant camera.

Inside the Mind of a Musician

It was a clear night so we got great footage of Times Square with all its lights, hype and glory. I expected to get pulled over any minute–two professional video cameras sticking up through a sunroof in the middle of Broadway seemed rather subversive, if not downright illegal–but we pulled it off.

Then more fun yesterday– filming Roy Nathanson's band kids at the Institute for Collaborative Education, then running over to Birdland for a couple hours to shoot the intro scene on their stage.

Gianni Valenti, owner of Birdland, was the only one gracious enough to offer his club for the film. As I told several club people, this is a demo product for students, and there is no budget for location shooting.

I was actually rather annoyed with certain club people–all the times that musicians come and sit in at their club for free, adding value to the club and making it an exciting place, but when it's time to give back, where are you?–not to mention the jazz educators and students ALL OVER NORTH AMERICA who are going to see this film and say "let's go to that club that was in the film!"

So when I hear whining from club people, like "well I have to pay someone to be here while you're filming"– especially when we've both been on the scene in New York for a quarter century and I knew you before you even had a club, and now you don't even have the vision to see that you must reach the students so that the audience for jazz music continues to grow AND your club can stay in business, and anyway you're at the club right now talking to me on the phone so why don't YOU be there while we're filming? but no, I guess you don't have that kind of vision, James.

Terry

So, because you dissed me like that, your club doesn't get an appearance in the film. All the other clubs do. But not yours.

I believe this is what's called "an executive decision." You make one, I make one. Checkmate.

SIX MILLION

In the Sunday Times Magazine of 1/20/08, there was an article titled "Art in the Age of Franchising" by Virginia Heffernan, detailing the "washout" of a TV show called "Friday Night Lights."

The gist of the article is that even though this show has a large and dedicated following, that is not enough to compensate for its lack of merchandising and online spinoffs, like all the other popular shows have.

But what really got me was this part: ". . . the show is a bona fide washout. Six or so million people watch 'Friday Night Lights,' compared with around 13 million for NBC's hit 'Heroes.' . . . In popularity, it lags far behind [some stupid sounding shows that I never heard of]. . . even now that the Nielsen ratings try to account for viewers who digitally record a show and watch it within a week of its air date, the show's numbers are lousy."

Lousy? SIX MILLION folks watching a show is LOUSY?

Excuse me. When did this happen, that six million people's votes don't count?

To put things in perspective: A Gold Record is half a million unit sales. A Platinum Record is 1 million unit sales. A Multi-Platinum Record is 2 million in sales.

So if 'Friday Night Lights' were an album, it would have gone Multi-Platinum three times already.

To appropriate a comparison from my favorite guru–we live in a world of zebras. The zebras like one thing, the lions (that's us) like another.

I guess that's why this blog, written for lions by a lion, has not been picked up by a major network for a new reality series.

Even with the writer's strike and all!

Well, if in today's zebra-world, six million people are nothing, lions can only bemoan their fate. Or not. Will you walk with me across the ruined savannah, slowly and with dignity, while we search for the meaning that makes life bearable?

CHIMPS VS. KIDS

While en route from one room to another, my attention was captured for a few minutes by a PBS program Gil was watching, about how humans learn.

The researchers showed some chimps a box on which they manipulated a few simple moving parts, after which a piece of candy would fall out of a slot.

They gave the box to the chimps, who copied what the researchers did, thus retrieving the candy.

The kids did the same thing in a separate experiment.

Then the researchers showed the chimps the same thing on a see-through box, where you could tell that the manipulations were unnecessary–you could just take the piece of candy out of the slot from the jump.

So the chimps cut right to the chase and did that.

But the kids went through the same process of manipulating the moving parts before extracting the candy!

The researchers were trying to prove that humans learn best by interacting with other humans and copying what they do.

In my own research, I have obtained the same results, however I interpret them differently: I say the experiment proves that humans will do the same stupid things over and over, just because they saw some other humans do it.

In the interest of science, I hereby donate these findings without expectation of remuneration, to my scientific colleagues who would like to make use of them in their own research.

JODIE FOSTER?

Today on the M train I saw a woman who looked EXACTLY like Jodie Foster. Was it really her? She had on a shlumpy cotton skirt and sandals, with an expired pedicure, and she was reading a paperback.

Um, maybe not.

GOOD NIGHT AND GOOD LUCK

Just saw it. Highly recommended. It's about legendary reporter Edward R. Murrow and his struggle to cover the news during the McCarthy era.

It's good to be reminded that this vile period of our history is more recent than some of us imagine. Blacklisting, slavery, the Salem witch hunts, Jim Crow, women's suffrage, the internment of Japanese Americans during WW II, and COUNTLESS other history bytes worldwide–up to and including today–prove that humans never tire of preying on their own kind.

An extra special treat in the Good Night film was the interspersing of the band scenes, with Dianne Reeves and quartet playing the role of a 50's jazz group. Dianne was in an "early Sarah" bag, and Matt Catingub plays fantastic Ben Webster-y tenor. I know him as an arranger and it was a pleasure to hear him play the horn.

I also like that the musicians credits rolled early, way before Key Grip and Assistant Wardrobe Assistant. Then they ran again at the end of the credits, right before the song credits. All great standards. The soundtrack is available on Concord.

PLAYING PUNDIT

For today's blog entry, I thought I would pretend to be one of those political pundit bloggers who blog while an event such as a Vice Presidential debate is going on. It seems fun and I've never done it, so I'll give it the old college try. Please be advised that my style may differ.

First off, the debate isn't on yet. I'm watching Hardball with that guy Chris. Don't know his last name, I don't watch TV hardly ever. Chris is interviewing a Democrat Congresswoman, a Republican somebody, and a pundit with a red tie. This is bizarre; it's like the pre-game banter of the hosts on a sports program. There sure is a lot of talk, talk, talk. Wonder who's in the locker room right now with the contestants–I mean, the candidates?

The show is taking place at Washington University in St. Louis, and there's a huge crowd of students in the background, holding up signs. My favorites: "Biden is hotter than Palin" and "HI MOM!"

"Countdown to the Debate"? What is this, New Year's Eve? The network ratings must be off the charts. I

Terry

wonder if they have this on in Farrell's sports bar on Prospect Park West, accompanied by beer and free popcorn.

I noticed a typical journalistic ploy–Chris had a list containing words like "composure, ideology, knowledge" and asked his guests to pick one that summarized what Gov. Palin would have to show tonight. But his guests were hip to it and they gave their own answers instead of filling in one of his ovals with a number two pencil.

Press hard. You are making three copies.

Boy, this political blogging is hard work. Especially when you're in the middle of baking acorn squash that has to be basted with butter and maple syrup during the baking process so it doesn't dry out.

We're also having sliced Jersey tomato in a dressing of fresh basil with olive oil and balsamic vinegar. In case you were wondering.

Back to the show! Now Keith O's program is on. I love how he does the parody segment with Bach's Toccata and Fugue in D minor as the theme song.

Well, I guess that's it for my political blogging today, because I'm kind of bored. And frankly, I'm worried about that squash. It sure has been baking for a long time, and it's still not done. I hope I didn't accidentally buy some of that genetically altered mutant squash.

Which reminds me, I haven't heard any of the candidates weigh in on consumer access to food supplements, the legality of food additives, and full disclosure of the pedigree of the food we buy and eat. Speaking of issues that are completely BI-PARTISAN, (lest I leave today's blog without dropping at least one byte of lingo) last I checked, everybody's gotta eat.

Inside the Mind of a Musician

TIMING IS EVERYTHING

The other night Gil was watching The Man Who Shot Liberty Valance, and I watched a little of it. The Valance character is played by Lee Marvin at his most despicable. Stoddard, Jimmy Stewart's character, is supposed to shoot Liberty Valance, so he waits for him to come out of the saloon. Stoddard can't shoot for shit, and Valance is a crack shot.

Valance, drunk, comes staggering out of the saloon calling for Stoddard to come out of the shadows so he can see him.

Because even in the Wild, Wild West there were standards in place, Stoddard comes out into the lantern light. It wouldn't be fair to be shooting from a dark corner.

Valance proceeds to play with Stoddard, shooting at his hat, and shooting Stoddard's right arm, his shooting arm.

Then Valance gets tired of playing and decides to end it. He says, okay, now it's right between the eyes. Very slowly, because he's so cocky and thinks he's in the catbird seat, Valance draws a bead on Stoddard. But because he goes so slowly, Stoddard–bad shot that he is–shoots Valance in the heart with his left hand!

The lesson to be drawn is this: never take your opponent for granted! Put another way, one could say–how is it possible for the rabbit to escape from the fox? Because the fox is fighting for his dinner, while the rabbit is fighting for his life.

Terry

ON THE ROAD AGAIN

ON THE ROAD AGAIN

Went up to Rochester on Saturday to play a gig with Jazzberry Jam at Club Venu. The hotel provided by the promoter was very un-happening. Specifically, the coffee machine in the room. Even more detail: usage is not recommended.

I press the "on" button on the coffee machine, but it doesn't work. Call up housekeeping. Guy comes up with another one. He's out the door in a flash, without waiting to see if it works. I plug it in. It starts spewing out leftover toxic sludge that immediately permeates the entire room with the most putrid, foul odor imaginable.

I put the coffeemaker out in the hallway. I have to call up the front desk FOUR times before someone comes up with an ionizer and air freshener spray. Keeping in mind, of course, that the air freshener was only marginally less toxic than the original odor.

Go down to the hotel restaurant while the ionizer is doing its thing. Order French onion soup.

Imagine my horror upon realizing that this soup is none other than the very source of the toxic sludge in the coffeemaker, which someone was evidently using to heat up leftovers.

If you were munching on something while reading this–my apologies.

Terry

THE PRINCIPAL IS YOUR PAL?

Not the one I saw today. Playing at a school in the Bronx with Blues Rock Connection, we parked our cars in the schoolyard where Richard, our leader, has been parking for the past 6 years he's performed there. A guy in jeans, a sweatshirt and sneakers comes by. "Move these cars."

"Um, excuse me, and who might you be?" I thought he was the custodian.

"I'm the principal of this school."

I almost said "and I'm Dolly Parton" but I restrained myself because I didn't want it to reflect badly on Richard.

The kids were all assembled in the auditorium with the show about to start, but this so-called principal was ready to cancel the show if we didn't move our cars RIGHT NOW! He even brought the security cop with him for backup! Well, I don't blame him for that. . . we ARE dangerous!

You know what parking is like in New York–Richard said "where should we move them to?" and this guy says: "That's your problem."

Lack of dress code aside (I mean, every school principal I ever saw was in a SUIT)–this non-gentleman still needs a serious attitude adjustment.

If any of you Board of Ed officials out there would like the name and address of the school in question, feel free to e mail me.

DRIVING DIRECTIONS

So today I had to play in boondocks.usa, otherwise known as Mendham, New Jersey. A woman from the office gave me directions over the phone yesterday. They were the type of directions that included superfluous landmarks and other unnecessaries. You know you're in trouble when

Inside the Mind of a Musician

halfway through they say "I know this sounds confusing, but..."

Oh, and halfway through them giving you the directions, they go back to about a quarter of the way through and embellish it, with much more detail, so that when you're driving and trying to follow the directions, you're not totally sure where the overlap is. "Is this the same right turn as two sentences ago?"

Street names? Forget it. It was more like, "Well, go down the road a ways, and when you see the dog lying in front of the brown house, turn right."

"What if the dog's not there?"

"You STILL turn right."

I can't believe I got there. I also can't believe I was the only one in the group who didn't get lost. Chalk it up to experience. And we won't go into too much detail about the time I was late to a gig IN MY HOMETOWN because after exiting for a Dunkin Donuts moment, I got back on the highway going west instead of east.

EAU CLAIRE, WI

Only one thing I didn't grok on this trip. How come you can't bring nail clippers on the plane, but the lady across the aisle had a ball of yarn and a PAIR OF KNITTING NEEDLES, big as you please.

Then the stewardess OH EXCUSE ME I meant flight attendant comes over with HER knitting to get some tips from this lady. Attention terrorists: your new battle cry may be "knit one, pearl two."

Terry

MY ANCESTRY

Sorry to disappoint you Geoff, but I am actually more closely related to trumpeter Clark Terry (at least, he calls me "Sis") than to either actress Ellen Terry or Civil Warrior Alfred Terry.

Check this out: One time I was driving to a gig in the Hamptons, a sumptuous locale known for its beaches, its rich and famous part-timers and full-time partiers, and its horrendous traffic. I left Brooklyn early in order to avoid the latter and possibly partake in the pleasures of the former.

When I finally reached the charming woodsy road that would whisk me to my destination at the rate of 25 MPH or less, I suddenly felt a bit peckish, and pulled over by a quaint country graveyard to eat my sandwich ("for tomorrow we may die...").

Upon finishing my repast, I decided there was time for a brief stroll amongst the gravestones, to see how old the place was. To my utter shock and amazement, half of the surnames on the stones were "Terry". It seems I had synchronistically stumbled upon the Terry family graveyard!

–But whoa there, they wuzn't my kin, son–

While I like the last name "Terry", and people hardly ever spell it wrong, it has only been my family name for two generations. My grandfather, Elias Tatarsky, came to New York City from Odessa, married my grandmother Nellie, and produced my Aunt Mickey and my father, Herbert. My dad was quite a smart fellow who excelled in the sciences. He decided that "Tatarsky" was too hard to pronounce, and he made the entire family become Terrys.

Perspicacious readers will note that my original family name indicates that I am a descendant of the Tatars, who eventually became mixed up with the Mongols and their boss, Genghis Khan. That's MR. Genghis Khan to you.

PULLED OVER FOR AN AUTOGRAPH

The other night I dreamt I was driving and a cop pulled me over. He was also giving someone else a ticket, and we were told to go into what seemed like the police precinct.

On a desk there was a book about jazz, with some pictures of me in it. Turned out the cop wasn't giving me a ticket, he just wanted my autograph.

Surely this is the ultimate meaning of the phrase 'in your dreams.'

ROAD RAGE

Driving on Rt. 80 today in the middle lane, this red SUV is on my right. I'm behind another car. The SUV speeds up and veers into my lane, cutting me off and forcing me to brake to avoid an accident.

Me no like dat.

So I switch to the far left lane to pass, catch up with the SUV, and look in the window. It's a blonde chick.

I have nothing against blondes. Some of my best friends. . . know some blonde people.

So after I gave her the Ocular Death Ray, I settled back to my normal driving rhythm.

But I continued to observe the blonde's movements– or rather, her vehicle's movements. And I noticed that she was cutting off many people, not just me. So it was nothing personal–she's just a Cutter-Offer.

Terry

Lord, give me the serenity to accept the things I cannot change; courage to change the things I can; and a case of light explosives to help me tell the difference.

THE FIRST TIME I SET FOOT IN ENGLAND

From an old journal:

On my arrival at Heathrow, there was no car to be found with my name on it. I went outside to wait in the taxi queue and called home. Turns out there was a message. I started to piece together that they thought I was coming tomorrow. Went back inside, found a driver from the same company and he called the office. Driver arrived within ten minutes. Good thing, too, because the fare must've been 60 or 75 bucks, it took half an hour and everything there was really expensive.

Looking at the scenery on the way, it was very nondescript. "Baltimore," I thought. No, not even Baltimore–three towns away from Baltimore. I thought it would get more interesting when we got near the hotel, but it looked like any city with chain stores and street construction.

Now I get to the hotel. Can barely understand the Indian guy at the desk. OK, I have to pay because the promoter's credit card only held the reservation. Dragging all my stuff to the lift. Trying to get it in the lift whilst holding the door and the gate open. Can you say "where's the f—-ing bellhop"?

The guy said 5th floor, there's no button for the 5th floor. I go up anyway. Don't see anything that resembles the number of my room, 23. Go back down. He says you take the lift to 4 and then walk up two flights. "With this?" I point to my bags. He comes up with me and takes the bags.

The room is the size of a walk-in closet. You can't get to the bathroom if the wardrobe door is open. I boil water in the decrepit coffeepot and make ramen that I brought from New York. Pathetic.

The room is so small that the remote for the TV is redundant. I unpack. Plug my Treo into the wall with my newly purchased UK voltage adapter. Thank the stars it works. I play Stan Getz and Billie Holiday to cheer myself up. It doesn't work.

I think to myself–I would like to like England. The names of the towns are creamy and thick, like "Cotswold" and "Devonshire."

I glance at the brochure for the hotel. Through the miracle of modern photography, it appears charming and spacious.

There's a part of me that wants to cry.

HOLY DAZE, BATMAN

Let's not talk about driving ten hours roundtrip in the pouring rain to visit relatives on Thanksgiving, shall we?

These are gigs, only you don't get paid for them. Pity.

One high point, though, was seeing my cousin Jason, who's about to graduate from U Mass with an astrophysics degree. So I mentioned to him that Jane Ira Bloom has an asteroid or something named after her, and inquired as to whether he might name his next asteroid after me. He said, forget asteroids–how about a planet?

Of course I said yes right away–I mean, besides Venus and the Moon, what other overtly female bodies do we have up there? More representation never hurts, right girls? So the very next planet that Jason discovers . . . well, let's just say, there'll be a lot of people eating crow.

The only downside is the likelihood that my planet will be located outside of our solar system, making visiting problematic, at least by conventional methods. But no matter: I have been practicing a few esoteric techniques (this is an example of what you can spend your time on if you don't watch TV, kids) that hopefully will allow me to travel to said planet anytime I want. Or maybe only on Leap Day, I'm not sure.

In any event, if you'd like to get in on the ground floor, as it were–just let me know. And a deposit never hurts.

ANTI-LOCK BRAKE SYSTEM

I do not like anti-lock brakes.

I do not like them, they feel fake.

(Trying to go with a Dr. Seuss thing here–work with me, people.)

The brakes are the only thing that I liked better on my old '91 Geo Storm GSI than on my current '04 Subaru Baja. When you apply the brakes over rough road surface, the ABS engages and causes the brakes to "chatter", or engage fractionally rather than totally. What used to be done by the driver's foot is now done automatically. This is a very disconcerting feeling, and it happens often on New York's third-world roadways.

I enjoy driving. I'm a good driver. I've got a clutch and I'm not afraid to use it.

So I'm not too keen on car companies deciding that drivers don't know how to brake and making the ABS a standard feature. Not keen on it at all. It seems like more trickle-down Big Brother legislation.

Oh, woe is me! But I must not sob; I will use my pen to cross out the slings and arrows of outrageous fortune! How about this bumper sticker: "My Other Car Is A Time Machine."

Maybe I'll transport myself directly to Dec. 21, 2012–do not pass Go, do not collect $200. Let's see what 12/21/12 does, because Y2K was a fizzle.

I just realized, the purported end of the Mayan calendar doesn't even have a snappy nickname! Must not have seeped into the collective consciousness yet. Must not have reached the Tipping Point. Well, be sure that I will weigh in on the subject in a future post.

Back to the subject of cars. I wouldn't want a car that "drives itself." (What–is the owners manual written in English, and Braille?)

Drivers of the world, UNITE! Let's put a stop the the Anti-Lock Brake System.

CAR RENTAL

I only had one weird experience in the rented Toyota Scion: While driving to my first destination, I noticed a certain Mazda in the rearview mirror. Drive drive drive, park, run an errand, get back in the car. Driving. Hey! The Mazda is still in the rearview! Am I being followed? Or does the mirror come with its own picture, like a new wallet?

LONDON CALLING

I was just looking through an old notebook in which I jotted down some infobytes while on a tour in London last year.

Terry

Did you know that the Waterloo Bridge is nicknamed the "Ladies' Bridge" (note correct usage of the apostrophe, Ms. Truss) because it was built mainly by women, during WW II. The part I like best about it is, it has built-in dynamite niches (I've got some of those myself) in case they had to blow it up during the war!

Unexploded bombs have been found in the Thames, and anytime something is built in the river they have to check for them.

BTW, the Thames is allegedly one of the least polluted rivers in the world (doesn't the word 'allegedly' have a delightful connotation?) although it is very muddy. It had originally been used as the city sewer, but was cleaned up in the 19th Century.

The Thames is a tidal river leading to the ocean. At high tide it rises 18 feet! Downriver is the "Thames Barrier," which prevents flooding.

There will be a quiz tomorrow.

REVENGE AT LAST!

Dig it: Me, Gil, Marshall, Harry and Zsa Zsa are cruising down Beneva Boulevard in Sarasota in the convertible with the top down. We're playing Cannonball on the stereo. Stop light–kid pulls up next to us blasting hip hop. We look at him and crank up Cannon. He rolls up his window!

WTF

Stuck in Holland Tunnel traffic, the lane next to mine was moving a little faster. A tan Mazda SUV drove by, blasting some rap which had "I wanna get my d--- sucked" as its main lyric. A woman was in the passenger seat, a man in the driver seat, and 4 or 5 LITTLE KIDS in the back, about 6 years old. I was unable to catch up to them to say "HELLO!??!!??! You're playing that in front of KIDS??!!??" I was so mad, I had to keep reminding myself that yes, Virginia, there really are idiots like that roaming around loose, with drivers licenses even. Sorry I didn't get the plate number, or I would post it here.

GAS

The thing is, gas is going up, so it costs more money to get to the gig. Traffic is going up, so it takes longer to get to the gig. But the gig still pays the same as it did before. You know you're in trouble when gas was $2.99 on the way to the gig, and it's $3.07 on the way back from the gig.

TSA=GOD

TV sets. They're everywhere. We're surrounded. They're all over every bar, every airport lounge, in public spaces nationwide. They're on the back of every airplane seat!

I just want to mention this: Whatever you look at also looks at you. "Remember '1984'" is my battle cry.

And don't get me started on airport security. The whole terrorism thing has certainly been a gigantic moneymaker for lots of folks–the government, weapons manufacturers, security companies of all sorts, and not to mention our beloved TSA, the Transportation Security Administration.

While the TSA ditzes around with their picayune regulations that do nothing to stop terrorists but are very effective at inconveniencing law-abiding citizens, I'm quite

Terry

sure that The Terrorists (hey, a mega-enemy that doesn't even have a border–it's better than the Cold War!) are having a good laugh.

You know you can't bring your own bottled water through the security checkpoint, so you have to buy a five dollar bottle of water from one of the airport vendors. Well, I can understand that. Water is very dangerous–it has hydrogen in it!

But if you put your bottle of water from home in the pocket of your cargo pants, well by golly, you can just waltz right through and they won't even notice.

By the way, starting next month there will be no more cash accepted for beverages, etc. on Jet Blue flights, so I'm sure that's happening on the other airlines as well.

Here we are at the beginning of a cashless economy. Remember what happens in the first chapter of Margaret Atwood's The Handmaid's Tale? (It's on the Powell's Bookstore list of frequently banned literature titles.)

Did you know that the American Federation of Musicians had to boycott Delta Airlines for a year because they wouldn't allow musical instruments as carry-ons? Every time I go to the gate, I pray they won't stop me. Airport security broke Valery Ponamarev's arm trying to take his trumpet away from him at the gate.

You can't check musical instruments unless they are in very special, expensive cases designed for air travel, otherwise they will be damaged and won't play upon arrival. Duh.

I think I may be coming to the end of airports. Besides, I've heard that travel broadens you, and I don't want to gain any weight.

By the way, I forgot to turn off my cell phone on the last flight, and discovered that T Mobile does not have service at 25,000 feet. Better start up those telepathy lessons again.

TORONTO IAJE

So I'm in Toronto today to give a presentation at the International Association of Jazz Educators.

Toronto seems like a nice city but I'm not getting to see much of it, at least not on purpose.

Yesterday, I'm trying to get from my hotel to the Convention Center, which is only a few blocks away. I follow the directions they gave me at the hotel, and I don't see anything that says Convention Center on it.

I go into a building and ask, and the guy says "Oh, it's right across the street." I go across the street and ask if this is the Convention Center, and this guy also says, "It's right across the street," only he's pointing in the opposite direction.

I go where he says, and again someone says "It's right across the street" and points me in yet another direction.

This happens seven or eight times, only about halfway into it, it starts to get a little more complicated:

"Go down those steps and follow the walkway, and it's right across the street."

"Go through that building to the end, follow the walkway, go around to the right and down those steps, and it's right across the street."

My amazing powers of deduction were leading me to believe that I might be getting further away from the Convention Center.

When I finally found it, I had no idea where my hotel was anymore. But when I walked back to the hotel with people who knew where it was, it was only 4 blocks away.

I took a good look at the entrance to the Convention Center before I left, so I would be sure to recognize it when I go there today.

If I might make a small suggestion to the city planners: perhaps the Metro-Toronto Convention Center could have a sign placed on it that says something like, "Metro-Toronto Convention Center."

But there's a Timothy's Coffee right on the corner, so I'm good.

As long as I don't pull a "Margot." She got lost in Tokyo by trying to use a ubiquitous fast food chain as the landmark back to her hotel.

She was rescued by the attentive staff at the distant hotel she ended up at after wandering the streets of Tokyo, when they made several phone calls evidently asking if anyone was missing a *gringa* from New York.

Well, at least they speak English here.

X DRIVING SCHOOL

I always take the secret shortcut to the Lincoln Tunnel from Jersey: from Route 3, take the Kennedy Blvd. exit at Toys 'R Us. Then follow the service road, otherwise known as 30th St. in Union City, to the tunnel.

Today a car cut me off on the service road. It was a student driver from the X Driving School (with a passenger who was, presumably, the instructor) according to the signs emblazoned on the vehicle.

I have to say, I'm really glad that there's at least one driving school out there that is teaching essential, practical skills such as cutting off other drivers.

A skilled cutter-offer will make a lot of progress on the New York Metropolitan Area's congested roadways. I applaud X Driving School of Union City, New Jersey, for adding this important skill to their curriculum.

SHOCK, DENIAL, ANGER, ACCEPTANCE

Today I went to the "hand" car wash on 4th Avenue, because my Subaru Baja was covered with some kind of slime and looked like hell. Totally unacceptable, as this is a vehicle that normally turns heads–and not because it's dirty.

Some of you know the car's story: I was Baja shopping on eBay (I had fallen in love with this model, but didn't want to buy or lease a brand new car) and when I saw this one I said "that's my car!"

My brother, who knows about cars, said I should bid on it.

Furthermore, he said that if I won it, he would pick it up for me (it was in Wichita) and drive it back! Lest you think my brother is some kind of saint, let me point out that he had a business trip coming up in Kansas, and he hates to fly.

Cutting to the chase, I won the bidding, and Zak, the seller, was fine with holding the car till my brother got there to pick it up.

Zak, by the way, is a big music fan who follows his favorite bands around (when I bought the car he was on his way to China to see someone's concert), and we stay in touch. He's trying to get me to play a gig in Wichita so he can come see me. But now that I think of it, if he went all the way to China, why can't he come to New York? Or PA, or

Terry

Jersey, or Illinois, or Florida, or one of the other places I'm playing in the near future? Hmmmmm.

(Note to Zak–dude, chill. I'm jus' messin' wit' ya.)

But enough about Zak. Back to the topic, which was the state of the Baja after it was hand-washed: still covered in what was evidently the result of a fly-over albatross with diarrhea.

Bummer.

I sought advice from the Guru of Google. A classic cars site said to use seltzer water without sodium. If that doesn't work, the next step is paint polish.

Well, I knew I had been saving that expired case of seltzer for something. I kept saying to myself, this case of seltzer is taking up space in the garage and I should get rid of it. But the pack rat in me resisted, and now I know why.

I used up the whole case of seltzer rubbing off bird feces from the hood, roof, trunk and sides of the Baja. Took me over an hour. I could have been practicing Giant Steps or engaging in some equally futile activity–but no.

During the course of the rub-a-thon, I discovered a secret weapon: you can use the cap of the seltzer bottle to add an extra bit of pressure to that stubborn Rorschach-like residue (tea leaves, anyone?) by simply covering it with the towel you're using, and rubbing away. Be sure to use plenty of seltzer so you don't scratch your paint.

Also remember that the bigger your car, the more bird droppings you may have to clean off of it from time to time.

Unless you have servants for that, which I could totally have if I wanted–but only if I lived in Port Au Prince.

EFFICIENCY, I LOVE IT

Eddie Caccavale told me a humorous story about road chops. We were doing a cabaret gig in Midtown, and he had just come from a rehearsal with Lainie Kazan, with no time to eat. He parked on Ninth Ave. at 6 p.m., but had to wait in his car till 7, when it would be legal to leave it. Our call was at 7.

Starving, Eddie gazed longingly at the Thai place that was right beside his parking spot. But he didn't dare leave his vehicle, even for an instant, because the traffic cops have iRadar.

He noticed that the restaurant had their phone number displayed on the door. He took out his cell phone and dialed it.

He ordered a Pad Thai. "Pick up or delivery," they asked.

"Delivery."
"Where are you located?"
"Right outside, in the gray van."

Once again, you can learn a lot from Eddie!

ELEUTHERA

I see that the island of Eleuthera in the Bahamas is approaching its heyday, after a long period of being off the travel-destination radar. The Club Med beach is supposed to be the best one, although the Club Med on Eleuthera closed several years ago. And I was there! In the 80's with Clifford Jordan's band. Melba Liston rounded out the horn section. Hugh Lawson was on piano, Paul Brown on bass, Wilbur Campbell, from Chicago, on drums. The gig was very easy,

Terry

we only played a few concerts, and the rest of the time hung out at Club Med.

Cliff arranged for us to do a free concert at a school for the townspeople, who were extremely poor. I remember the look on Hugh Lawson's face when he tried the piano they got for us, because only about 3 keys out of 88 worked.

The weather was not that great. We were on the outskirts of a minor hurricane; it rained every afternoon, as it often does anyway in the tropics. One guest that we were palling around with had flown there in his private plane. The weather wasn't to his liking, so he split.

The island of Eleuthera evidently lost its allure in subsequent years, and returned, for the most part, to its former low-key, unspoiled state–thus attracting those who appreciate the mellow island life. Lenny Kravitz goes there several times a year, between tours. He says " I bring one pair of pants, a couple of T shirts, and no shoes." Hey–me too! At one point, my one pair of shoes (brown leather Docksiders–Cliff made me get them shined at the airport and it completely ruined their appeal, but they did look better onstage) was stolen on the beach. So I just went without them for the rest of the week. I got a cheap pair of sneakers at a local store when it was time to fly back home to New York.

Or was that the other Club Med, the one in Guadeloupe?

One day Cliff went to the nude beach, wearing only fins, mask and snorkel. I don't have a picture of that, except mentally.

There are lots of other stories–mainly unprintable, at least in a free blog. (With ever an eye toward future commercial exploitation, we trudge onward. . .) Oooo, that sailing instructor. . .

Ah, the Eighties! An era that so badly wanted to be the Sixties, but was born too late. "Just say no" had not yet been invented, and sex, music and uncontrolled substances wended their way through the expanding universe, ensuring that the world would continue to turn.

Until the Nineties, when everyone joined health clubs and started just saying 'no' a lot.

And now, from our 'aught six vantage point, we can simply smile and say, "I'm glad I was there."

Or was I?

Terry

OSAMA HATES JAZZ

Inside the Mind of a Musician

OSAMA HATES JAZZ

You heard right: Osama bin Laden hates jazz. He hates it because jazz music is about Freedom, Democracy, and non-discrimination (if you can play, we don't care what the heck you look like.)

Attention Loyal Americans (and other International Democraticians): if you want to show your loyalty to Democracy and the American Way, STOCK UP ON JAZZ RECORDS NOW! Or else play into the hands of Osama and his henchmen! Your choice!

I was ruminating the other day: Supposing somebody–a civilian–is hanging out over in the Middle East somewheres, and this person happens to run into Osama, like, in a bar on the Army base or something. Well, maybe not in a bar. Maybe out at the camel trough. Outside of the Officer's Club. (If you are hiding from the Army, the best thing to be is the custodian at the Officer's Club). And supposing this person says to themselves, "Hey, I could pop old Osama off right now and have done with it." And WHAM, they do it.

Now remember, this Osama dude is a guy whom the U.S. is doing its level best to hunt down and bring to justice, or else hunt down and destroy, whichever comes first. But they can't seem to find him. So if some civilian finds him by accident and offs him, Good Samaritan-like, then that person would be a hero, right? WRONG! That person would be arrested! Because that's how Justice works.

CALL FOR MUSICIANS

Derwyn Holder and I have noticed how there seems to be less work for wedding bands, so we are starting a divorce band.

If you are interested in auditioning, please know the following tunes: Let's Call the Whole Thing Off, Breakin' Away, Mercy Mercy Mercy, My Attorney Bernie, After You've Gone, Freedom Jazz Dance, I'm Still Standin', The Masquerade is Over, That's All, Stormy Weather, Once I Loved, I'll Get By, You've Changed, Diamonds and Rust, Everything I Have is Yours, If You Could See Me Now, There Will Never Be Another You.

TONIGHT'S GIG

Tonight I played my first commitment ceremony. I was a commitment ceremony virgin, but no more. Actually it was basically the same as a wedding. It was a thirty-something couple, and they wanted a lot of songs from the 90's. Unfortunately, the 90's was not our best era, musically speaking. There was this one song–the progression was C, Cmaj7, C7 . . . and guess what chord comes next? Why, Cmaj7 of course. Everyone knows that C7 resolves to Cmaj7. Sheesh. Who are these people writing this crap? If you're out there, listen up: C7 DOESN'T EVER GO TO Cmaj7. EVER. GOT IT?????

ELEVATOR MUSIC

Interesting gig today for a Fortune Magazine private event. I played clarinet in an elevator for a couple of hours! When people got in, I asked them what they would like to

Inside the Mind of a Musician

hear for the next twenty seconds. Luckily no one said "silence."

Here were some of the requests: Girl From Ipanema, New York New York, Summertime, The Candy Man (she remembered playing it on bassoon in high school), Benny Goodman. My big number was "Bess You Is My Woman Now"; that really took 'em to the top in style.

Discussing w/ my colleague Seadog (aka Jenny Hill) why it is that the classical sax players are STILL putting down the jazz sax players. Jealousy, my dear, plain and simple. Because the fact is, WE CAN DO GIGS AND THEY CAN'T!

I believe if you're a musician, you should be able to play by ear w/ no written music, and be able to improvise. Call me old fashioned, but I also believe that artists should be able to draw, doctors should be able to heal, and waiters should be able to remember my order long enough to get it to the kitchen.

FAKE KING COLE

In a restaurant today they were playing some music on the system that sounded like a guy trying to imitate Nat King Cole. He got some of the inflections right, but when I listened closely I could hear it wasn't the real thing. Plus, the soloists were not up to the standard that NKC associated with. All in all, this music represented the main problem with much of today's popular music: it attains nothing short of the Zenith of Mediocrity. And it does it very well. So well that most people can't tell the difference. Unless, of course, you hear it side by side with the real thing.

As Wm. Shakespeare said a few years ago in 'The Merchant of Venice',

Terry

"The crow doth sing as sweetly as the lark
When neither is attended, and I think
The nightingale, if she should sing by day,
When every goose is cackling, would be thought
No better a musician than the wren."

BARRY'S BDAY

I think the folks at Camino Sur, over on the West Side, were a bit overwhelmed by the turnout for Barry Harris' 76th birthday party. Even the owner was out on the floor working, there were so many people. I can imagine the conversation at the club the night before: "Yeah Joey, you can take off tomorrow night, it's only a jazz group."

The band featured Richard Wyands, Earl May, Leroy Williams, Charles Davis, Roni Ben Hur, and Damian on tenor. Dave Glasser and Nat Jones sat in, and so did I along with Bob Cunningham, Henry Grimes, Kiane Zawadi and Tom on tenor (hey Tom I can't find your card–please send me your number again.) Before that, I sat in on DRUMS and played with Sam Dockery!

Tardo Hammer and Larry Ham were hanging out, and Eddie Locke. Eddie was telling me what it was like to play in Coleman Hawkins' band. How cool is that?

The party went on till the wee hours, and yes, the huge cake was entirely consumed.

EVERYTHING IS RELATIVE

Deb: whatcha tryin' t' do girlfriend–fry my brain? Too late though–it's already fried to perfection (if not to a crisp.)

Inside the Mind of a Musician

You're asking me about rules; now, let's see, I've got the Jazz Rule Book right here. . . hold on a sec. . . OK, here it is–Rule #115, Paragraph 12, Sub-Paragraph 5.3, Clause 8:

"Learn the rules, then forget them."

So you see, it's useless to ask me about the rules. Also bearing in mind that when they say "forget the rules", what they really mean is "break the rules." But my personal favorite stage is the next one: NO RULES! Here's the catch: the only way to get to NO RULES is to pass through LEARN THE RULES and BREAK THE RULES first.

Are you following me?

But seriously, Deb, you are welcome to come over to the studio and take a lesson with me at my usual fee, whereupon we shall sit down together and review my old college music theory notebooks. Provided we can read my handwriting.

Oh, and here's the other thing: it's weird to talk about rules for chords, because as Einstein discovered, Everything is Relative. You take a group of three or four tones, you can make several different chords out of them depending on what you set as the root. Similarly, several seemingly unrelated chords can actually be the same chord if you know the Rosetta Stone (she was the cowbell player) that ties them all together.

All this is not to discourage you, because you are on the right track. As I intimated earlier, a thorough knowledge of the rules of music is a prerequisite, albeit not the end point, for true musical creativity. But if all your software needs to do is come up with the changes to Puff the Magic Dragon, then all this may be overkill.

And as The Oracle might say, what's really going to rock your world is the ultimate stage: BACK TO THE

RULES. If you want to hear what that sounds like, I have two words for you: Barry Harris.

JAM SESSION ETIQUETTE

Hey, miss would-be vocalist–was it absolutely necessary that you cut off Tom Glusac's burning solo on Night and Day in order to sing the melody not that well? And was it also absolutely necessary that you sit there and gab gab gab to your boyfriend, loudly, during the rest of the session? Oh, it was? I beg your pardon.

AND ANOTHER THING

Talking with Tim Price today about how jam sessions are nowadays. Apparently there are still some instrument-holders out there who don't realize that when you get up on stage to play, you're supposed to know the song.

Furthermore, if you can't hear the changes to 'Little Sunflower' and have to read it out of the Real Book onstage, please be under the age of thirteen.

Jam session players: Maybe you don't know every single change, but please know at least the MELODY and the FORM of the tune, or don't play. You're ruining the experience for the rest of us.

Macho tenor players: please do not morph the end of a song into an *a cappella* version of Giant Steps.

Female singers: unless you are Cynthia Scott, Vanessa Rubin, Nancy King, or someone AS GOOD AS THEY ARE, please just listen and try to learn something.

SAVING THE BEST FOR LAST

Two months ago I bought Miles Davis Quintet Live in Stockholm, recorded in 1960. It is a classic among classics in live recordings. My copy is still in the shrink wrap. Like a fine champagne or box of imported chocolates, I seem to be saving it for the right occasion–perhaps some cold, gigless night of the future.

Or perhaps I am cherishing the feeling of the night I first heard it. Records like this must always be listened to at night. The starkness of day dulls the senses; it makes the ear divide its attention amongst the goings-on of daylight. No! Bring on the night, with a creature comfort by your side: a glass of port or cup of Lapsang Souchong, wafting sultry scents to awaken the finer sensibilities. Or, an actual creature–cats make good listening companions. Humans don't. They talk too much.

It would be nice if the last thing you heard before you died could be Miles' solo on Blue in Green. It would be nice if the last thing you'd ever see could be a Caravaggio, and not a print of a bad watercolor on some hospital wall. It would be nice if the last thing you smelled could be a rose. It would be nice if the last thing you tasted was a fresh strawberry, instead of blood. It would be nice if the last thing you touched would be someone you loved.

But this world ain't that nice.

ONCE MORE, WITH FEELING

After my Hartford masterclass, several students wanted to talk with me individually. One of them, Mark La Rosa, plays tenor and guitar in a band, and he gave me a home recording of some of their tunes. On listening to it, I

Terry

was impressed with how much feeling and expression they put into their music.

Technique, musical knowledge, repertoire–these things can all be learned. But you can't learn feeling. You either have it, or you don't.

I'm continually surprised by how many professional musicians I come across whose playing lacks the passion that would seem to be requisite in this field.

In my view, the arts are fields for personal expression, so if you're not going to express, you're just cluttering up the field.

The cream rises to the top with TRUE artists: those who put forth their personal expression that is SUPPORTED BY EXCELLENCE IN THEIR CRAFT.

The expression alone is not enough; the craft alone is not enough. But when these two aspects meet, mountains can move and walls can crumble.

Too bad a lot of folks can't tell the difference between cream and low fat skimmed milk.

Are their ears on a diet?

TOP GUN

If you happened to be walking down W. 57th Street in New York last Monday night, and you saw that huge throng of people through the window of the Steinway piano showroom (where no one rested their drink on the piano) and wondered what was going on, I'll tell you. That was the annual Nola Recording Studio soiree. If you are a recording musician, and you were not out of town or in bed with the flu, then you were there.

Inside the Mind of a Musician

Nola is a legendary studio, presided over by Jim, Johnny and Billy, the reigning monarchs. I've recorded several albums there.

This is such a great party, musicians make a point of going to it every year. It's not the food–giant Dune-like sub sandwich, pasta salad, shredded carrots–nor the free drinks–wine, vodka, basic mixers–that excites us. Rather, it is that ineffable camaraderie that exists when you are amongst high-level colleagues–flying fighter aircraft, winning the World Series or being in the studio wrapping up tracks after the first take. It's like belonging to an elite club. And it's a club you can't buy, fake, or _____ your way into. It is a complete meritocracy.

You get to hear some interesting gossip, too! For instance, I learned that tenorman Frank T. is sitting on more than ten CDs worth of unreleased Coltrane, recorded live at clubs in the 60's. Now, to a jazz musician, that's like finding out about buried treasure. Pure gold! But evidently Frank has not been able to secure a recording deal for these tapes, because no record company will finance it. They won't finance it because they will lose money on it!

So probably the only way for these tapes to get released is for some jazz-loving private sector tycoon to pay for it.

Just as I was getting ready to leave the party, I start talking to Adam Rafferty, whom I know via Mike Longo. Then Ken Hatfield sees us and comes over, and I end up staying for two more hours.

Ken had a lot of interesting things to say, relating to his belief that serious musicians should insist that their music be listened to seriously. He was like–no ringtones, no background music. Just put on the disc, sit down, and listen to it. He feels that musicians need to band together on this issue, and not allow their music to be thrown into the ring with all the other mediocre and less-than-mediocre music out there.

I'm reminded of Derwyn Holder's theory: he says that we should start jazz sessions in some remote cabin in the woods, with "Keep Out" and "No Trespassing" signs all around. Eventually, the local youth will hear the music and start coming around to listen. Pretty soon, they'll be clamoring to be let in.

If I can get my band members to come play with me in a remote cabin in the woods every day for no money, then I will definitely do it.

It might be easier in New York though. I can see it: we have a very low-key storefront downtown. Outside, a velvet rope and bouncers. Or maybe nothing. Just the music happening inside. But the door will be locked. Yes. The bouncer will be on the inside–you don't get in without a password, Our friends and fans will have the password, so they can come anytime they want. Pretty soon, the general public will be clamoring to be let in, at any price.

Private Sector Jazz Loving Tycoons Apply Here.

I'LL HAVE TO GO WITH DESTINY ON THIS ONE

In a previous post, I put forth Derwyn's idea about playing jazz in a cabin in the woods, with No Trespassing signs all around, until the local youth follow the sound of the music and clamor to be let in, at any price.

Well, it turns out that this is not what Derwyn had in mind AT ALL! His idea is that of a Jazz Monastery, where the music goes underground, like the forbidden manuscripts of ancient times, and is nourished in secret by devoted generations of Jazz Monks, only to surface again in a future era. Hardly the 'marketing ploy' that I was envisioning. How utterly crass of me. But I can't help it–I was a victim of society!

So is jazz music destined to become the Holy Grail of musical legend? Only time will tell. . .

If jazz is destined to become a secret transmission that will die to the present day only to rise again in a new world, then so be it.

I could always become a short order cook. People gotta eat.

Chauffeur? Dog groomer? Personal shopper?

If only more people realized that they need food for their soul as well as their body. Music cuts straight to the core. But only if you listen to it!

COOL VS. DORK

You have to admit that the saxophone is a very cool instrument. That makes sax players cool by proxy.

Or maybe it's the other way around. We're cool, so we play sax. Otherwise, we would play some dorky instrument, like bassoon.

JUST KIDDING!

Now you'll think I'm joking, but this is a fact that I found out today:

Vivaldi (Antonio, the Four Seasons guy, yeah, him) wrote THIRTY SEVEN bassoon concertos.

This begs the question, why.

Terry

FEINSTEIN'S

I finally figured out how to pronounce it–both syllables rhyme with 'wine'. Or is it 'whine'? No dressing room! Again! Of course, the star gets a room in the hotel (as does the Musical Director), but the rest of us make do with a back room featuring an endless parade of waiters and busboys tromping through with tables, chairs and piles of napkins. They are all handsome Latino guys in elegant uniforms. Matadors for the moneyed class? For what is their job if not another sort of bull-fight.

My colleagues in the band have to come in through the kitchen with drums and amps. But with my woodwindy portability, hell, I blow right in through the front door.

This must be the big time they promised me. I'd know it anywhere.

Stephen Holden from the Times gave us a good review today, that's nice. Haven't seen Rex Reed's review yet; he was there opening night, sitting with my friend Ann Ruckert, so I got to meet him.

Unfortunately for you impecunious buckaroos and buckarettes, Feinstein's is beaucoup bucks. As my friend and colleague Richard Frank just wrote to me:

"I've listed one of my kidneys on Ebay, and if I get a good enough bid in time, I think I can afford to come see you at Feinstein's!!! See you in a little less elegant setting in a week or so."

The 'less elegant setting' he refers to is a school gymnasium. As Richard is fond of saying, "I started out 40 years ago playing in school gymnasiums–and look how far I've come!"

Inside the Mind of a Musician

THESE ARE THE GOOD TIMES

On a record date, some of the guys were complaining about doing a lot of takes on the tunes.

I was like, you know what guys? When you're 95 in a nursing home eating applesauce and watching Jeopardy in the day room, you'll remember back when you were making records in the studio and say, "those were the good old days."

SITTING IN

My dear friend trumpeter/composer Tom Goehring was playing last weekend at the Deer Head, so I went. No sooner had I sat down than I was invited up to play, and with the cast that was onstage, I did not hesitate!

Tom on trumpet, Vic Juris on guitar, Gene Perla on bass, Michael Stephans on drums. I played the rest of the night with them. At one point we were playing either What is This Thing Called Love or Confirmation, I forget which, and I ended my solo with some figure.

I stood offstage with Tom and listened as Vic began his solo. He took my ending lick and repeated and elaborated on it. "He liked my lick!" I said to Tom. "Yeah," he replied, "how does it feel to have a friggin' genius take your lick and make a whole chorus out of it!"

HAROLD VICK

At the IAJE conference I picked up a CD reissue of Harold Vick's recording "Watch What Happens" from the ejazzlines.com guys, who had a booth set up with some of the CDs and DVDs from their catalogue. We talked about Harold, who Rob and Doug consider to be under-recorded.

Terry

This particular recording, from 1967 on RCA, features Vick with a small ensemble arranged and conducted by Ed Bland, and a rhythm section of Herbie Hancock, Bob Cranshaw and Grady Tate. Need I say more?

I will say more. I want to tell you a story about Harold that he told me many years ago. When I met Harold, he had already survived two heart attacks, the second of which he flatlined after. He was clinically dead. He told me that while he was on the operating table and they were trying to revive him, he was already on the way to the next world. He said he was on a sort of road, and he came to a fork where the road divided. He heard music coming from one of the directions, so that's the fork he took. Then he woke up back in his body. I remember so clearly how he said "Su, I've been following the music my whole life. So when I heard that music, that's the way I went."

One time Harold told me he had just turned down a one-nighter in Switzerland. I was flabbergasted. I would've taken it in a heartbeat. But Harold was well over six feet tall, and he didn't want to fly in coach for eight hours, do a gig, then turn around and do another eight hours back. Now that I'm not 25, it makes perfect sense to me.

Harold was a snappy dresser, by the way. He and I used to make fun of these green polyester pants that James Spaulding would wear.

After Harold had the second heart attack, the doctors told him he couldn't play anymore. But he started to practice a few minutes every day in his apartment, without telling anyone. He was a player–what the hell else was he going to do? One day Shirley Scott was visiting him, and after she left he started to practice a little. But Shirley had forgotten her scarf, and she came back and heard him practicing. She said "You don't have to practice by yourself–I'll help you."

And she started coming around and playing with him, till finally he was back playing like his old self.

Harold Vick died in New York in 1987. He was 51 years old. I miss him.

MY OWN STUFF

My butt has been kicked many a time by stuff I wrote myself!

It seems that the "compositional mind" and the "playing mind" do not always run on the same track.

I always say that when you're performing, your job is to interpret the composer's music–whether the composer is Monk, Stravinsky, Boulanger, Pete Seeger or you yourself. That way you remove your ego, your tummy ache, or thoughts of your mother in the front row from the equation and are able to focus on the music.

That said, I think what drives many players is a wish to interpret the sounds they hear in their heads, and/or hearts. This can be done through playing or writing.

When you're writing, it's like time is slowed down, and you can write something that might even be too hard for you to actually play, and you have to practice it to get it. This has happened to me many times, and I think it's a good thing because it helps me grow as a player.

Being a composer also helps when I'm playing someone else's original music. In these situations, I use my "compositional mind" to plumb the depths of new music that has not received the benefit of the repeated performances over time which help to solidify its interpretation.

Terry

MY LATEST IMPROVISATION

I'm really grooving with the painting project now. For the finishing touch I will put a small, five foot shark-fin shaped blue piece (Hemlock) which will fit between Tuscany and the Pacific Rim. (Bet you didn't know they shared a border. . .) I improvised the whole thing, starting out with only a basic idea of somehow dividing the space into 3 sections.

When I was living in Hartford with Dave, Lisa, and Jerome, we used to cook using what I called the "Zen Method." If you were cooking asparagus, how do you know when it's done? It's easy if YOU ARE THE ASPARAGUS. Can you dig it?

My college fascination with Zen extended to a little canon from Kodaly choir that I put lyrics to:

"One thing that's required, is eat when you're hungry, sleep when you're tired, just this–"

That's all it was, just five bars. We were given it in solfège originally, of course. All our teachers were from the Liszt Academy in Hungary, they could solfège ANYTHING. Talk about musicianship.

I was classically trained, starting on clarinet when I was 9. My first instrument was the accordion though, from age 5. I always loved music, but I think I was afraid to become a classical musician because I didn't think I could memorize pieces. So I took the easy way out, and became a jazz musician. HA!!

I always had this sense of The Art of Improvisation being something that was applicable to life as well as music. It seemed like a good skill to develop, growing up in a chaotic universe. (I'm not talking about my home life. I'm talking about THE UNIVERSE.)

Inside the Mind of a Musician

And now that I've been studying this art for over thirty years, I find in a way it gets harder, not easier–but it also gets a lot more fun.

Sports share this improvised quality with jazz. You have a basic game plan (the tune), but unpredictable things happen while you're playing that cause you to alter your trajectory.

The other thing that athletes share with performers is the intense training that goes on behind the scenes. Then you bring the focus and intensity of training to the game, or the show.

The best part, for me, is to keep pushing the envelope of creativity. How far can I go? How far can I go and still come back?

Some players evolve so much over time that their fans can't always keep up. You hear a lot of people say how they dig EARLY Trane or EARLY Miles. Then there's cats who started out Out, and gradually came back in—like Pharoah Sanders. Maybe that's like those particles in physics that go backwards in time. Neat trick.

COUNTRY MUSIC DOES NOT NECESSARILY SUCK

I recently joined My Space, and the best thing about it, for me, has been getting turned on to lots of good music. A whole lot of sax players from around the world have signed up to be "friends" with me; in case you're not a MySpacer, that means having a cyber pen-pal, except you don't ever have to write.

Also, a lot of die-hard music fans troll My Space for new music. Since I don't "approve" any "friend requests" until I go to that person's My Space site and check them out

(I can't be "friends" with just anyone, now can I?), I get to hear whatever music tracks that person has posted on their site.

One of these music fans had the music video of "Prayin' for Daylight" by Rascal Flatts on his site. I played it and really dug it, the hook is off the hook! So I bought the song from iTunes and was playing it in my car today, over and over. It reminded me of when I was thirteen and listening to David Cassidy singing "I Think I Love You" about a hundred times in a row.

TRUMPET PLAYERS

Playing with a new trumpet player is like a blind date. It could be great, but it could be miserable. When it's miserable, the only consolation is that you're getting paid. But when it's great, like it was last night, it's like heaven.

I've played with hundreds of trumpet players, and believe me, there are not that many who–in a horn section–can play in tune, have good phrasing, know how to blend, and know how to listen. And not play too loud.

In order to make the arrangements (which are often written by a non-horn player) come alive, the horn section also has to play the correct articulations, and they must do this AS ONE UNIT.

How you attack a note, when and how you cut it off, embellishments like glisses, scoops and turns, when to play softer or louder, diminuendo or crescendo, when to lay back, when to play on top of the beat, how to phrase in different styles of music (swing, bossa, Afro Cuban, Salsa, samba, reggae, funk, rock, shuffle, and the list goes on)–these details separate the Horns of Wheat from the Horns of Chaff.

Inside the Mind of a Musician

Since I had just played a gig with trumpet ace Scott Wendholt, I was a little spoiled. But Ross Konikoff was super, a joy to play with. Come to find out he tours with Liza Minnelli, among others.

He was easy and fun to play with. Plus, he knows how to make the appropriate sarcastic comments (this is de rigueur for a trumpet player, but optional for a sax player) at the right time.

Timing is everything, you know.

I always thought it must be a gas to play with a small, super-tight horn section like in Tower of Power.

I've seen T of P numerous times, but my favorite time was standing backstage in the pouring rain listening to them at the Pori Festival in Finland, about ten or eleven years ago.

Man.

JVC JAZZ PARTY

I was invited to the JVC Jazz Festival opening party by Russ Dantzler from Hot Jazz, so I went. It was on the lawn of Gracie Mansion, which is supposed to be where the Mayor of New York City lives, but it isn't. I guess Mr. Bloomberg didn't take the gig for the mansion that comes with it–he already has a mansion.

The food was very good. I had salad with rice and shrimp in a delicious sauce, and did not spill any on my new white shirt.

The band was great! Saxophonist Sonny Fortune had his quartet, and my friends Steve Johns and Chip Jackson were on drums and bass.

After the gig, Chip was telling me some great stories about playing with Elvin (Jones, not Smith). He also related a story Billy Taylor told him, where Billy was sitting with

Terry

Art Tatum listening to a student play a transcription of one of Tatum's solos. Afterwards, Billy asked Tatum what he thought of the performance. Tatum said, "Well, he knows what I played, but he doesn't know why I played it!"

That cracks me up!

Then Chip and I were discussing how students tend to play repertory music just like that–they know the how of it, but not the WHY.

I think most players eventually get the WHY just from growing up, and gaining life experience. The WHY is certainly not taught in any of these fancy jazz colleges, not because it can't be taught, but because there's just too much focus on the how: What scale to play over what chord, and all that jazz.

I like to teach the WHY, and I have certain exercises to train for it. If you pick up the next issue of Jazz Improv, my column deals with one of these exercises. But the main responsibility lies with the player. It has to do with going deeply into the source of the music, and that is much more about energy and emotion than it is about what scale you should play in measure 18.

ELLINGTON & STRAYHORN

Practically the only solace in having to get up at some ungodly hour to do a school concert–or some other task having to do with 9 to 5 reality–is listening to radio station WKCR from Columbia University. I believe they stream live on the web if you're not in New York. The other day they were playing The Queen's Suite by Duke Ellington and Billy Strayhorn, a remarkable piece that was recorded as a SINGLE PRESSING that Mr. Ellington sent to Queen

Elizabeth following her elegant and courtly reception of the orchestra at Buckingham Palace.

The Queen Suite was not released to the public until after Ellington's death.

It's clear that Duke could never have written this piece without Billy Strayhorn.

The relationship between Ellington and Strayhorn has been well documented elsewhere, such as in David Hadju's Strayhorn biography, so I need not go into it here. But in a nutshell, I think there's no question that Strayhorn's writing had an immense effect, particularly on Ellington's later writing. This suite is packaged with two other suites composed solely by Ellington–notice how Strayhorn's writing continues to influence Duke even years after Billy's death.

The album is available so check it out.

JAM SESSION PROTOCOL

Being that I've been attending a lot of jam sessions lately, I thought I would give the younger players a crash course on how to make a good impression on your colleagues, as well as the audience.

Rule Number 1:
Don't play too long. As Art Blakey said to me once (after I played three choruses on Stella instead of two, which would have been proper), "Don't play too long, or people will be applauding 'cause you're through!"

Rule Number 2:
If you don't know the tune that is called, and you don't hear the changes–don't sit in, sit out.

Rule Number 3:

Respect the style of the session. If the cats are playing tunes and bebop, don't come in squeaking and squawking with your avant-garde, conceptual vibe, ending in the middle of the chorus because you don't know the form. Don't go into a jazz session and call "Funky Chicken." Don't go into a blues session and call "Giant Steps." Etc.

Rule Number 4:
Horn players–the rhythm section is not your personal Jamie Aebersold record. Try out all your licks in retrograde inversion at home. We're trying to make some music here.

Rule Number 5:
Buy something to drink. Support the place that's hosting the session, especially if the only people in the audience are the musicians.

Follow these simple guidelines, and your jam session experience will be greatly enhanced, guaranteed! See you at the session. Seven Steps to Heaven in 7, anyone?

CARING FOR THE NOTES

You have to care for each note.

What do I mean by that?

Every note and phrase is like holding an egg or a little bird in your hand. You nurture the notes, because they come to life (or not) depending on how you play them.

Whether we play a note loud or soft; how we attack the note (tongue, slur, breath attack, accent, ghost note, scoop, bend, etc.); how we cut off the note (short, long, held to full value, *diminuendo, sforzando,* etc.); the feel of the phrase (swing, straight 8's, on top, in the middle, or behind the beat, etc.); matching the pitch of the lead player, blending with the section, or if you're the lead player you have to

Inside the Mind of a Musician

establish all of these things so the other players can follow you.

These are just some of the things that we do for the music that is in our care.

Without the players, music is just black marks on a page. Even if you can hear music in your head–the reason you can hear it is that you've heard musicians play. The ways that you have heard musicians play, in your experience, will define your standard of how music should sound.

Whether listeners or players, we should always remember that no music exists without players to play it.

I daresay our planet would be well served by imagining the source point of many other things.

How did this salad get on the table? Because some trucks drove lettuce and tomatoes there and people put prices on them and put them on the shelves.

Before that, some folks had to build the trucks and drill for the oil to make the gas to fuel them.

Let's not forget the farmers who planted the lettuce and tomatoes and the workers who harvested the plants.

And the sun and the rain that enabled the plants to grow.

And the bees!

And how did the sun get up there anyway, and whose idea was having rain, and why do bees have stripes?

Well, that's enough thinking for today I think.

Terry

DIGGING THE ZEITGEIST

Inside the Mind of a Musician

DIGGING THE ZEITGEIST

Yesterday at the gig, Mike was talking about how good the blood oranges are that he got from Fresh Direct. I said, yeah–but if you order food on the Internet then THEY know what you eat! Mike said he doesn't care if THEY know what he eats. Now keep in mind, Mike will not get EZ Pass because he doesn't want THEM to know where he drives his car. So I said, yeah, but on the day when THEY want to implant the chip in you and you don't go, and you have to go underground because that is what you'll have to do if you don't get the chip. Then you'll be a fugitive and you won't be able to go in a restaurant while you're on the run from the law, and order what you like to eat. Because THEY will know what you like to eat because you ordered it on the Internet!!!

During this conversation, Brian had no comment because he was cracking up.

Mike laughed and I think he's starting to see my point.

But in a larger sense, I think it often happens that one sacrifices one's principles for the sake of convenience. I definitely do.

AS THE RATWHEEL TURNS

People, if you like the new album–please tell someone, or buy a few more copies as gifts. We're trying to make a living over here! Do you know how many times my chihuahua has to pee on his electrolyte newspaper pad to generate enough power for me to get on the Internet for an hour? Why, some days, when there's a lot of e mail, I even have to feed him potato chips!

ON THE TOWN

Last night Donna Dennis and I got together and went to a swanky cocktail bar called Pegu Club in the Village. It's modeled after the Officers Club of the same name in Rangoon that Rudyard Kipling describes in Sea to Sea.

Watch the bartender make the drinks–the detail is extraordinary–right down to squeezing the lemon so the oils mix with the liquid in just the right way. Fun place to people-watch too.

Then we walked over to the Blue Ribbon and had a great meal. There were "identical twins" seated next to us wearing the same clothes, the same glasses, even sporting the same iPhones.

At the end of the meal I asked them if they were really identical twins, and Donna chimed in "I think you're not!" They said they are artists and this is part of their act. Their name is Andrew Andrew.

When they left, the people at the next table leaned over and said, "What did they say? They wouldn't talk to us!"

HUMOR, THE 7TH SENSE

This whole thing with the Muslim cartoon controversy is really something. Normally I refrain from blogging about political subjects (as if there is anything that ISN'T political) because others are better informed and do it far better than I. But certain things do jump out and demand a comment, do they not? Anyway, it's certainly one of the

Inside the Mind of a Musician

main functions of the comedic realm to explore the limits of bad taste.

I think the main problem with organized religions is that very few of them have any sense of humor. (Hence the veritable cornucopia of priest/rabbi/minister jokes–they make good targets.) Some exceptions might be certain Buddhist sects. I have observed the Tibetan Buddhists, for instance, to display a humorous bent. For instance, when they make those statues out of Yak butter, and then sit around and watch them melt. Hey, you gotta love that.

I have heard the Dalai Lama speak in person several times. One time, at a monastery in New Jersey, he commented how amusing it was that everyone stood up when he walked in. It's like, when you have the big picture from the top of the mountain, you can see how funny a lot of things are, when they are not funny at all down here on the ground. I'm sure the Dalai Lama doesn't think it's funny that well over a million Tibetans have been murdered and imprisoned by the Chinese government. But I doubt if he would let a cartoon about it ruin his day.

A sense of humor is probably the sort of thing no one wants to admit they don't have–it's sort of embarrassing. Unless they don't care, which is entirely possible. We feel sorry for the No Humors, and they probably feel sorry for us because we are so foolish.

It seems that people who take a great interest in the foibles of humans either become psychiatrists, or comedians. But psychiatrists have the highest suicide rate of any profession. Because they have no outlet. Unless they moonlight as comedians.

Do you know the story of The Great Gilliam? I'm paraphrasing it from Ouspensky, or Gurdjieff, I'm not sure.

Terry

It seems that there was this man who was very depressed. He ended up at the office of a certain psychiatrist and said "Doctor, I'm so depressed. I have been everywhere and tried everything. You are my last hope. Please help me."

The doctor said, "I have just the cure for you. You must go see the funniest man alive. His name is The Great Gilliam."

The man sighed deeply and said, "Doctor, if that's your advice, then all hope is lost. I am The Great Gilliam."

RAT WHEEL RULES

1. ALL RATS ARE RESPONSIBLE FOR OILING THEIR RAT WHEELS. THIS WILL BE DONE ON THEIR OWN PERSONAL TIME.

2. RATS MUST KEEP THEIR WHEELS IN MOTION NO LESS THAN 95% OF THE TIME.

3. ANY RATS CAUGHT NOT MOVING THEIR WHEELS FOR THE REQUISITE AMOUNT OF TIME WILL BE SKINNED, AND THEIR HIDES USED TO MAKE SOCKS FOR THE OTHER RATS .

4. RATS ARE NOT PERMITTED TO SOIL THEIR WHEELS.

5. A RAT WILL NEVER BE MENTIONED BY NAME AFTER ITS DEMISE.

WHAT'S THE POINT

Sometimes when I'm ruminating on the pointlessness of most human endeavors, I think about the immediacy and the life changing (and life ending) consequences of war, as experienced by the young soldiers who are engaged in it. From my middle-aged vantage point, they are just kids, and they are being thrown into a surreal situation that calls upon the most profound human abilities. If you've been following the news, you know that that many of the soldiers are coming back with injuries that will alter the course of the rest of their lives. Many of them, in the past, would have died from their wounds. But modern technology is often able to save their lives, meaning they must adjust to a life without a limb, or with brain damage, or another severe handicap.

I think it's important for any individual to understand what it is that she or he can contribute to the world. My gift happens to be music so that's what I do.

I think everyone has a special gift. It may not have anything to do with your "job". But I believe that it's every person's responsibility to find some way to contribute positively to the planet. Unfortunately school doesn't help much with this.

GAME OF LIFE

My 6 year old niece said "Will you play Life with me?" I said, "we're playing life right now." She said "no, the game." So we played this board game called Life that had zero relevance to actual life, teaches no skill, requires no intelligence beyond that of Cro Magnon man, and states that the winner is the one with the most money at the end of the game. Huh?

I don't play board games, except for Scrabble with my aunts every other Thanksgiving. And chess about every five years. But now I'm getting an idea for a game. It's called

Terry

Feudalism. You pick a card designating you as a Lord, Vassal, Peddler, Pilgrim, Soldier, Bishop, Serf, Blacksmith, or Merchant. There will be various pitfall cards drawn along the way. My favorite: "Get dental work." Whoever makes it to the age of 40 wins. I know, I know, it needs development. Feel free to do it yourself and send me a small royalty, so I can have the most money when I die and be THE WINNER.

OBJETS DE MUSIQUE; IDENTITY CHIPS W/ DIP

Reading about the latest art-world phenomenon in Leipzig: art students have been going there for years to study traditional painting–learning things like draftsmanship and perspective. Paintings by those all-grown-up-now artists are now at the top of the lists of art collectors worldwide.

How can a Composer/Musician (is this anything like a Philosopher King?) tap into the international collector scene? The very things that make music sublime and ineffable (1. an existence that unfolds in time; 2. a mode that bypasses the quotidian cognitive center and rushes right to the emotional center; 3. the element of rhythm that connects one's own pulses to those of the surrounding universe AND THESE ARE JUST THE ONES OFF THE TOP OF MY HEAD) make it highly unsuitable as an expensive object in a collection. I don't care how out-of-print that vinyl side is, it ain't gonna fetch half a mil at Sotheby's.

For those needing consolation at this point, follow Step 2 below. All others, please proceed to Step 3.

Step 2: Repeat this mantra: Price is only a thoughtform. . . price is only a thoughtform. . . price is only a thoughtform. . .

Step 3: So here's my idea–a Musical Talisman. This would be like a Collector ring tone. The Talisman's shape is similar to a locket, and may be worn around the neck or carried in a pocket, or displayed in one's home or elsewhere. It contains holographic images, music of the Collector's choice (perhaps composed especially for the Collector–that brings the price up) and whatever else they'd like, up to the gigabyte limit. You could even have it on a chip that is implanted in your body, kind of like a 4-D tattoo.

Here's a tangential trajectory I can't resist: It's probably only a matter of time before U.S. citizens will be required to have identity chips implanted. Did you know that a lot of people are doing this already–on a volunteer basis–and storing their medical records on the chip?

But I say, why stop with Social Security numbers and medications? Is my entire existence to be summed up in a number and a med list? No, I protest! I want it on the record: I dig Miles Davis! Sarah Vaughan is my favorite singer! Giorgio de Chirico is the bomb! Long live Zhang San Feng!

Yeah, put all that on my chip.

Whew.

Anybody got any extra Soma?

CELLPHONES ARE THE NEW CIGARETTES

My theory that cellphones are the new cigarettes is based upon my latest observations.

On public transportation, walking down the street, in bars, and even at home, people are obsessively playing with their cellphones. Especially now that the phones also take photos, play music, keep calendars and play games with you.

Terry

And a cellphone is even better than a cigarette, because it's legal to use it in a restaurant. Not polite. . . but legal.

Just don't take it out on the airplane–but you can't smoke on a plane either.

And you can be sure that using your cellphone will not contribute to the risk of getting lung cancer–although brain cancer may be another matter.

I definitely prefer cellphones to cigarettes. When I was in college, I tried to take up smoking, but was unsuccessful. I would buy a pack of cigarettes, but then I'd forget to smoke them.

So now if you're waiting around for your date to show up, instead of lighting up, you just whip out the old cellphone and play a game of Zap, or look at the pics you took yesterday of your friend's dog.

Or if you feel nervous about something, instead of reaching for a smoke, you can text your psychiatrist.

Speaking of nerves, the other day I was shopping for vitamins and came across the Bach Flower Remedies, which I'd been hearing about for years but never tried. They are tinctures that you dilute in water to cure nervous tension. Everyone in New York has nervous tension.

So I got a vial of Hornbeam, which helps with procrastination and anxiety about tackling new projects.

It works! Whereas before, I felt guilty and anxious about my procrastination, now I feel perfectly fine about it!

SCHUMANN RESONANCE

Sound is everywhere. It was the first thing ever created. It ain't called The Big Bang for nothin' ya know!

Every sound has a vibration, or frequency. A sound vibrates a certain number of times per second; we use the term "hertz" (hz) to indicate this vibratory rate.

Our planet Earth has a frequency that is created by standing waves in its electromagnetic field. A definition from Wikipedia: "The Schumann resonances (SR) are a set of spectrum peaks in the extremely low frequency (ELF) portion of the Earth's electromagnetic field spectrum. Schumann resonances are global electromagnetic resonances, excited by lightning discharges in the cavity formed by the Earth surface and the ionosphere."

There's lots of information on the Net, some of it quite geeky. But the point I want to make is that you don't have to buy the $99 CD that one "healing" website is selling in order to listen to the Schumann Resonances. You can easily hear some of the higher "overtones" of the 7.8 hz fundamental by downloading a free tone generator and listening with earphones on your computer.

The various websites seem to differ on the exact frequencies of the overtones, but if you go for 33 hz. you will experience a beautiful, calming, earth ELF for free. Those of you who haven't been in the music business for thirty years can probably go even lower.

Enjoy!

JUST WONDERING...

If maybe, possibly within my lifetime [although I will not be able to benefit from it because I will be too old to play, but the younger musician sisters could] that some visionary concert promoter could take it into her or his head that women instrumentalists don't necessarily have to be grouped into a "Women in Jazz" anything, that they could even, (I know this is really going out on a limb) have a woman instrumentalist in the same spot as a man instrumentalist, and maybe, just maybe, this would become (gasp) standard practice.

PUBLIC SERVICE ANNOUNCEMENT

Talk to your kids about jazz. Before it's too late.

TRIBES, ETC.

Getting serious for a moment (in great juxtaposition to most of these entries, ICYHN) I share the view that present political incompetence and abuse of Planet Earth will eventually bring about drastic change (as if it hasn't already). The animals known as humans will find themselves in far fewer numbers, and will need to form tribes or gangs in order to survive. So maybe we should all start thinking about who we'd like in our tribe.

As a musician, I have often thought about my role in society and in the universe. Music is an extremely powerful force, and musicians are the arbiters of that power in a social context.

Macrocosmically, music is a product of the universe, and as such is subject to its laws.

I believe that this perspective will come in quite handy when humanity finds itself regrouping into tribal units.

{When they reprint this entry in The New Yorker, the editorial comment will be, "huh?"}

DATED, SHMATED

I wonder what the obsession with "new releases" in music is all about. It's great (sometimes) to hear something new, but the musicality, artistry, swing and depth of past releases that have become classics should not be undervalued as a result. People need to listen to the music (i.e. content), not the medium. Marshall McLuhan's buzzphrase "the medium is the message" has become too true for our own good.

This sort of thing doesn't happen in the art world. I mean, does anybody ever say:

–What do you think of this Rembrandt?

–Oh I don't know, it's a little dated.

STILL THE SAME OLD STORY

I was just glancing at the jazz listings in the New York Times weekend arts section. There are twenty six groups listed. Guess how many are led by a woman? One. Guess how many have any women in the group? One.

Gee, haven't we come a long way.

I want to remind everyone that CONSUMERS HAVE POWER. If you want to hear me and your other favorite players (of any gender!) on the radio, call up or e mail the station! If you want to see us in club and concert venues, e mail them and say so!

Ten years ago or so, there were no "health food" products in the supermarket. Now, there are entire aisles devoted to "healthy, low-carb, protein this 'n that, organic" etc. etc. Why? Because consumers demanded it!

YOU HAVE THE POWER. USE IT.

YOU HAVE THE POWER...

Terry

THE END OF CHRISTMAS

I played a school gig this morning with Blues Rock Connection, and the first assembly was all kindergarten and first graders. Since our usual program is for slightly older kids, and involves discussing the evolution of blues and rock in the context of social and political history (the Civil War, slavery, segregation, etc.) we decided to forego that and play mostly holiday songs for the little ones. We did songs like Jingle Bell Rock, Blue Christmas, Y'me Hanukah, Feliz Navidad–so we thought we pretty much covered it as far as political correctness goes, and the kids loved it.

Then the principal comes up after the show and says that normally it is school policy that no holiday songs be sung, so nobody feels left out.

So Richard says, well what do they sing, then?

And the principal says, they sing songs about winter.

Well. That ought to suit the PAGAN community in Rockland County just fine.

Then Richard mentioned he's been trying to write a song about Kwanzaa, but he couldn't think of a rhyme.

You know me–never one to shrink from a challenge! So I wracked my brain almost the whole way home, and I finally thought of one:

Kwanzaa, schmanzaa.

But I was still only at the George Washington Bridge, so to put the rest of my driving time to good use, I started on a limerick about the unusual name of the place we were playing.

It goes like this:

"There was a young lady from Tor,"

Well GOODNESS ME, look at the time! Gotta run, y'all!

Inside the Mind of a Musician

HAPPY HOLIDAYS TO ALL SENTIENT BEINGS!

THE NEW YEAR'S GIG

Once upon a time, there was a staple of the musician's financial diet, known as the "New Year's Gig." In days of yore, New Year's Eve could be counted upon to supply players with not just one gig that would pay January's rent, but also a bunch of others that one could dole out to one's friends, Santa Claus-like, in grand style.

Of course, the days when New Year's (for short) paid a month's rent were over long before I arrived in New York toting my sax case, but I've heard tell.

In my day, NYE (for shorter) usually paid around double what a regular club date would pay. (A club date, for the uninitiated, means a private party, like a wedding, bar mitzvah or dinner dance. In Boston, they are known as "GB gigs"–for "general business." On the West Coast, they are known as "casuals.")

The last hurrah of the traditional NYE was Y2K.

Are you still with me?

I'm referring to the New Year's Eve of the year 1999 going into 2000. Remember how lots of people said that the computers were going to revolt because their programming didn't go up to 2000? Remember all the dire predictions that were made about the inevitable failure of anything operated by a computer?

Y2K, lest we forget, was the catalyst for lots of city dwellers to chuck it all and move to remote areas of the country, sometimes to underground structures that would supposedly withstand not only the perils of Y2K, but also any nuclear events, foreign occupations, or global warming

77

Terry

catastrophes that may come about. This is not a joke, it really happened.

I may be starting an underground taiji dojo slash jazz club in Montana, by the way, if anyone's interested. (Jon Tester–if you're reading this, I just want you to know that you will get in free.)

But back to NYE of Y2K. I, personally, was a little trepidatious about putting my car in a parking garage that night, in case it became trapped inside and I couldn't get home. Ever try getting a cab on New Year's Eve in New York City? But as it turned out, the Fear Alert churned out by www.nyc.gov, aided and abetted by Channels 2, 4, 11, NY1, WINS et al– served to curtail traffic to such a degree that I GOT A FREE PARKING SPACE RIGHT IN FRONT OF THE NATIONAL ARTS CLUB AT GRAMERCY PARK, where I was playing.

The gig paid in the four figures. Low four figures, but still. It was fun, it was a jazz gig. Then, after the gig: no traffic, no problems. And we all woke up on the day after Y2K, and absolutely nothing happened.

But something did happen. The computers went ka-flooey, and DELETED ALMOST ALL THE FUTURE NEW YEAR'S GIGS from the year 2000 on.

And that's why, boys and girls, there are no more New Year's gigs.

Oh sure, there's the occasional exclusive private shindig, or E flat hit in the Village. But I'm talking NEW YEAR'S EVE HERE! What happened to the days when I led a big band at Tavern on the Green, and made up funny patter on the mic, like "It's two minutes to midnight. Don't worry folks, this watch was calibrated by NASA!"

Well, maybe you had to be there. And I was.

Inside the Mind of a Musician

SO, YOU WANT TO BE MY "MY SPACE FRIEND"

A while ago, Tim Price sent me a CD in the mail, and on the envelope he wrote "Let's dump the 'Sweet' stuff–ha!", referring to the moniker that was bestowed upon me by my dear departed friends and mentors Cliff and Junior, as well as by the very much alive and swinging Barry.

Of course, as the late jazz pundit Marc Crawford once pointed out, the name "Sweet Su" refers not to my personality, but rather to my sound on the saxophone.

This relieves me of any responsibility to uphold the characteristics of a person deemed to possess a "sweet" personality by the world at large. But anyway, now that Tim has given his official permission for me not to be sweet anymore, I have really been cutting loose. For instance, I had a wonderful "take this job and shove it" moment earlier this week. It was great. And the latest one is my new MySpace blog entry, which I am reprinting here in its entirety:

SO, YOU WANT TO BE MY "MYSPACE FRIEND"?

Greetings, cyber angels and devils, and those who have not yet declared their position. Please be advised that I will not automatically click "Approve" on your friend request. Here's the deal:

If I know you and you are my friend or I otherwise admire you from afar, I will click "Approve" without necessarily visiting your page first. Life is short.

If I don't know you, I will go to your page to see who you are. After checking out your page, I will return to my Friend Requests and click "Deny" if any of the following conditions apply:

1. I think your music sucks.

Terry

2. Your other "Friends" are all scantily clad women in various provocative poses.

3. You have too many "Friends." I am not here to become a statistic on your behalf.

4. All your Top Friends are really famous people. Because, dig it: all my Top Friends are actually my friends, famous or not, and I like it that way. By the way, if you find yourself getting edged off my Top Friends list, don't be sad, it's just that MySpace is becoming so popular that every time one of my dear friends adds me, then one of my other, more recent, friends may have to share the space for awhile.

5. You have one of those secret profiles that only a Friend can view. Classic Catch 22: I can only view your profile if you're my Friend, but you can't be my Friend unless I view your profile.

6. I can't get your music to play. I will give you a few chances, though. But it may take awhile.

7. I just feel like it.

8. You are dead (in which case I somehow feel that MySpace will not be your preferred mode of communication) or else masquerading as a famous dead person, in which case I don't know who YOU are, and in any case, even if the person you are "representing" is one of my heroes, he/she has obviously not been complicit in the Friending process, and therefore it's a moot point, isn't it?

So if you still want to be the "Friend" of such an obviously arrogant, conceited, elitist bitch, try me!

MUSIC–AN AURAL TRADITION

Our world is becoming more and more visual. Meaning that we modern, human, urban-dwelling creatures are taking more and more of our reality from what is seen, rather than what is heard. Or, for that matter, what is felt, tasted, and smelt!

In an article by Jeff Hull in a recent Sunday New York Times Magazine, this idea is explored in terms of the other creatures surrounding us on the planet. (Surely you did not think we were alone?) In fact, since humans are surely in the minority, creature-wise, we may well take a look (there we go again) at what other critters are up to these days. Are they downloading videos along with their music?

In his article, Hull profiles 'sound architect' and archivist Bernie Krause, who for twenty five years has been making field recordings of everything from ants to elephants. "Every organism has an acoustic signature," Krause is quoted as saying. His hypothesis is that an animal's evolution depends upon its ability to choose a habitat in which its mating call can be heard over the din of urbanization and industrialization—not to mention the mating calls of the other creatures around it.

What does this mean for us? Merely this: with the advent of the downloadable cellphone ringtone, humans have acquired a new way to broadcast their mating calls!

Even though I already have a mate, if I heard Charlie Parker's "Koko" on a ringtone, that would definitely get my attention. Of course, my ears would perk up even more if I were to hear one of my own compositions. Yessirree bob, if I heard "Terra Incognita" or "Gilly's Caper" on someone's ringtone, I simply wouldn't rest until I called Harry Fox to make sure I got paid for it!

Terry

My friend Saul Rubin, a great guitarist who plays in my band, talks about students who come to him for lessons. Some of them, he says, want him to teach them some "jazz licks", or they ask him to teach them some amazing line that he happened to improvise in a solo on some gig that they saw.

Saul's response is "if you want to learn jazz, I have three words for you: listen to jazz."

Jazz is a form of music. Music consists of organized sounds. It is a "hearing art." Although music can be symbolized on paper, its meaning unfolds via the aural pathway. It has a secondary meaning that is acquired through its vibrations, which can be felt by the body. If the visual sense is used at all in the appreciation of music, it is only as a distant third.

Although we often use visuals to "enhance" the music, the fact is, you don't need to see anything. The music itself provides all the information. When properly attended.

Perhaps this is World Government's great plan: to increase the bombardment of its citizens with more and more images that go by faster and faster, till we're trapped on a great ratwheel of advertisements. If we tread without ceasing, our reward might be—an increased credit line!

Music cuts through to the emotional core of a person. That's why crying babies are soothed by lullabies; why stutterers don't stutter when they sing; and why wartime composer George M. Cohan was awarded the Congressional Gold Medal.

Music has the power to create, and to destroy. That is why it is loved, and feared. That is why you owe it to yourself to just sit down and listen.

Inside the Mind of a Musician

SORRY, WE'RE CLOSED

"Sign" of the times:

THE UNITED STATES IS CLOSED FOR RENOVATIONS. WE WILL REOPEN IN NOVEMBER UNDER NEW MANAGEMENT. WE APOLOGIZE FOR ANY INCONVENIENCE.

The pundits are now admitting we're in a recession. Another "sky is blue" story, eh?

So I do a school presentation last week on the Upper West Side, heretofore assumed to be one of the "better" neighborhoods. The brightest kid in the class was a girl about 9, who said her dad plays the saxophone. We said, who's your dad? Turns out we know him, fellow by the name of Dave.

Meanwhile, Andy and Sheila (both of them sax players) moved to Vienna two years ago with teaching positions. They have a great apartment and full health coverage. THEIR daughter–same age as Dave's–is fluently bilingual if not trilingual by now, while Dave's kid is surrounded by numbskulls in what passes for public school education in this country.

No wonder musicians are flocking to those doctoral programs like there's no tomorrow...

there's no tomorrow...

there's no tomorrow...

IF CONSTRUCTION SITES WERE BROADWAY SHOWS

–Hey Joey, guess what! I just landed the role of Particulate Supervisor in "Hamilton Avenue Underpass"–that should run five more years at least!

Terry

 –Hey congratulations Sam! Boy, "Ground Zero" has been running so long, I'm gonna put my kid through college on that alone.
 –Yeah, and José just told me he's goin' in to sub for Manny as Sheep Run Man on "Alice Tully." And he's gonna make the extra bread as a walker for Backfill Guy.
 –Ya know Sam, I always say 'thank you' in my prayers for havin' jobs that run eight years whether they're successful or not.
 –Yeah me too. And when they close, there's always another one! But if ya get offered Crane Operator, don't take that–it's jinxed.

ZEITGEIST, REDUX

 I lived in Germany for half a year in 1996-97. I was doing a show at the Tanzbrunnen Theatre in Cologne. It was a really good original show with an onstage band, and it featured musical numbers interspersed with comedy sketches–a German "Saturday Night Live", if you will.
 One of the stars of the show, Markus Profitlich, was signed to do his own TV show right after we closed.
 Markus did his routines in the Cologne dialect, which is to German as Yiddish is to Hebrew. So my minimal skills in German were completely useless in deciphering what Markus (we called him "Profi") was saying. But Profi was so funny that he could make you laugh even if you had no idea what he was saying!
 One of the cool things about living in Germany was studying the language. There is a great German word for which we have no English equivalent, so we just use their word: Zeitgeist. When pronouncing this word, say the first

letter like "tz." That's how they say it in German, and it puts the zing into it.

"Zeitgeist" is usually translated as "spirit of the times." The literal translation is "time-ghost."

In today's New York Zeitgeist, I notice an article on page C5 of the business section: "Listing Top Jobs but Charging Candidates to Seek Them."

President Bush's proposal to privatize Social Security has had an interesting trickle-down effect. I first noticed it on screening services for musicians and composers, where you had to pay a fee to submit your song to a music festival, television music supervisor, or record company. In other words, instead of the company paying to look for the talent that THEY NEED IN ORDER TO STAY IN BUSINESS, they have the TALENT pay THEM!

Around the same time you started to see this concept in the area of health insurance–an area where costs were skyrocketing and companies started making THEIR EMPLOYEES pay a percentage of it.

As our population grows, more and more costs, in widely disparate fields, are being passed on to individuals.

Zeitgeist.

On a personal note, as an artist, I feel that while I cannot help being influenced by the Zeitgeist, this is not my aim at all.

In my music, I seek to express principles, ideas and feelings that are not limited to the spirit of any particular age or any particular nation–but rather are universal and timeless.

Terry

BROOKLYN SERENADE

Inside the Mind of a Musician

BROOKLYN SERENADE

When I'm home in Brooklyn, I'm usually composing music around 6 pm. Every night at 6 the Mr. Softee guy comes up my block and sits there with that stupid theme song blaring at top volume, until I go out and signal to him to turn it down, which he does immediately. That little 6/8 ditty is very annoying, especially the *ritard* at the end, I really hate that.

So yesterday I went out and said "Dude, how about when you come down this block, you just turn it down automatically so I don't have to keep coming out here?"

He gave me a big smile and said "Yes, but I like to see you!"

NEGOTIATING

Lying around my studio was an old cassette series on the art of negotiating, by a fellow named Roger Dawson. It was in a really nice portfolio case, with the shrink wrap still on it. I opened it, and started listening to the series in my car (yes, my 15 year old car has an actual cassette deck, remember those?) The series is really good. So I was listening to it, getting all fired up for the next chance I would have to negotiate something.

Sure enough, today in Brooklyn I passed by the flea market they have every weekend in Park Slope. My eye gravitates toward a tan, fringed leather jacket with handmade wooden buttons. It was so cool. I've wanted a leather fringe jacket since I was like, 10. (It was the same thing with my tattoos. I wanted a tattoo since I was 10–so when I was 34, I got one.)

Terry

Anyway, the lady says "Well, I wanted $100 for it. But I'll take 80."

"I don't think I can do 80," I say.

"Well, I can come down to 75. But that's the best I can do on this, it's handmade."

I reviewed in my mind some of the tactics Roger Dawson taught: Don't display desire. When you hear the price, you should cringe. Be ready to walk away from the deal. String them along, don't agree to the price too quickly.

"I'll take it," I said.

"By the way," I asked, "where did you get the jacket", thinking she would tell me it was from some Native American reservation somewhere.

"It was lying around the house," she says. "I have a big house."

I wear the jacket home, and as I'm taking it off, I notice a price tag on the inside, from a second hand store about fifteen blocks down the street. The price was clearly marked: $39.95.

The last thing Roger Dawson said was: "No matter how good a deal you may have gotten, you'll always think you could have done better."

TO KILL A MOCKINGBIRD

Recently I was coming home to my block in Brooklyn and hearing bird calls coming from a tree in front of my building. This was happening almost every night, from about midnight on. At two in the morning it was still going on. It was all these different bird calls; I figured one of my crazy neighbors somehow put a remote controlled recording of bird sounds up this tree. It sounded really fake, because obviously there wouldn't be all those birds up in the tree, taking turns singing their different songs one after the other. It was loud. It was the middle of the night. My annoyance knew no bounds.

So today I saw our handyman outside. "Jack, who's the joker with the bird calls" I said. "No, that's a real bird," he replied. "It was driving me crazy!"

Evidently Jack's attempts at slingshotting the creature have made the habitat somewhat hostile, and the bird has thankfully taken up residence elsewhere.

IT'S MY BLOG AND I'LL BITCH IF I WANT TO

I don't know why I had to pick Saturday afternoon to try on hats with ear flaps at Dave's Army Navy in Park Slope. If I didn't know taiji, I would've been crushed by the relentless throng that was passing between the ditzy rearview-sized mirror and the cash register.

And the clerk: "Did you make your decision yet?" Hurrumph. Do you think I did not notice the insolence of your persnickety, final adverb?

IS IT MY FAULT YOU'VE GOT A BIG SELECTION?

STRIKE UPDATE

Coming to you from Brooklyn, where one can while away the hours in one's own little neighborhood, and never know that there is a transit strike going on that has New York City paralyzed.

Except that my students cancelled because of the strike. I was also going to go into town to do Christmas shopping, which is, of course, out. Oh well. As Robert Burns almost said, the best laid plans aft done gone agley.

But hey, we have plenty of shopping right here in Brooklyn, don't we, Deb? I will patronize my local establishments. Better to contribute to the Brooklyn economy anyway, in preparation for the Secession.

THE VIEW FROM BERNSTEIN'S GRAVE

I almost missed it. I was looking for something a little more grand. After walking all around where it was supposed to be and not finding it, I realized that only rich people have giant funereal monuments erected for themselves.

Artists, on the other hand—if I may speak for us all—prefer to spend our cash on the finer things of life, not death.

So I started to look for a plain, simple stone slab in the ground. And verily, his name rose up to meet mine eyes. He's buried in a rectangular, grassy spot between Battle Path and Liberty Path, next to his wife Felicia Montealegre Bernstein and his sister Shirley.

My neighbor Marcia used to come to this graveyard to rescue lost cats and such. She told me one time she went to Bernstein's grave, and Harvey Keitel was standing there, paying homage. So when I started out this afternoon, I brought a pen, just in case Harvey Keitel was here and I could get his autograph. But he wasn't, so I'm writing this instead.

Behind the graves is a little monument bench displaying the Bernstein family name. When you sit on it,

Inside the Mind of a Musician

your back is to the graves, and you are then treated to one of the most lovely views on earth. Green-Wood Cemetery is full of incredible views.

In front of you and to your right is the polished gray granite monument of one Otto August Badenhausen. To the left, the Jackson obelisk-with-the-top-chopped-off, apple blossoms strewn around its base and the grass beyond, from a 30 foot high apple tree.

Being Spring, there are blossoms and newly-leafed trees everywhere you turn. This is the highest point in Brooklyn, and beyond every hillock and glimpse of paved path, more hillocks can be seen, all dotted with grave markers from the sublime to the ridiculous.

This high ground, complete with landscaping, water features, and on-site wildlife, is the best real estate in New York City. If you're willing to pay the price.   ***PUN-BLOCKER HAS BLOCKED THIS PUN—TO VIEW SEE BELOW***

The view from Bernstein's grave is his final composition. Moreover, when you feel compelled—and you will feel compelled– to come around back and sit on this here bench and take in the scenery, it will hit you: the son-of-a-gun is still conducting his hind-parts off.

***People are dying to get in here. BadaBOOM.

EPISODE 23

This is a synopsis of Episode 23 from the "I'm Mad As Hell And I'm Not Going To Take It Anymore Chronicles":

Terry

Woman goes into hardware store and begins perusing garden hose connections. Young male clerk approaches: Can I help you?

Woman: Yes, I need a connector from the hose to the sprinkler.

She shows him which sprinkler she bought yesterday. He examines it, looks like he has no clue. Probably is barely old enough to drive, let alone set up a sprinkler in his parents' backyard. Goes in the back to ask one of the men. Comes back with a know-it-all attitude, even worse than before.

Young man: This is what you need (shows her a brass fitting)

Woman: This doesn't look right.

An exchange follows, during which the young man interrogates the woman, Gestapo-style, about the kind of hose end she's got. The woman (in the throes of an upper-respiratory something-or-other and not feeling too well) gets more and more confused, as he shows her more hose connections, none of which seem to be the right one, and capping his demo off with:

"If you don't know what kind of hose you have, then I don't know what kind of hose you have."

This last bit is said in the most arrogant and condescending way possible.

Woman: Look. I've been shopping here for six years, I've spent hundreds of dollars in here. The last thing I need is some smart-ass punk like you talking to me like I'm an idiot. You could learn something from one of your mentors here, who at least ACT like they don't mind answering what may be stupid questions, and they do it with a smile. If you can't be bothered to speak to customers in a civilized way, then

Inside the Mind of a Musician

you shouldn't be in retail. So why don't you go back behind the counter and try to observe and learn something.

Woman receives a standing ovation from the four or five other men working (of course they were already standing up) and is then helped by one of them, graciously and with a smile. She leaves, satisfied with her efforts (small though they may be) to rid the earth's atmosphere of a bit of excess testosterone.

I THINK I MIGHT BE IN THE WRONG LIFE

It's a late afternoon in summer, and I'm at the Subaru dealer in Bay Ridge, getting my truck fixed.

Why am I not on the deck of my beach villa, tanned and windswept and briefly clothed, sipping a lemonade?

I think this same thing every day at this time, even though I can count the times I have sipped lemonade on the deck of a beach villa on one hand.

Lemonade?

It reminds me of an old New Yorker cartoon: two robed and past-middle-aged monks are standing on the terrace of the monastery at sunset. One is saying, "It's been twenty-five years, and I still think of this as the cocktail hour."

Remember when you stood on the corner of Cropsey Ave. and Bay 17 waiting for your truck to get fixed?

Remember that day on the beach in 1984?

Remember when you could still bring toothpaste on the airplane?

Terry

THE CUSTOMER IS ALWAYS WRONG

And now for the latest "The Customer Is Always Wrong" Prize, awarded to TW Cable for their excellence in the following categories:
1. Most Service Outages
2. Longest Telephone Wait-time
3. Best Inescapable Telephone Loop System
4. Most Inefficiency
5. Best Excuse For Not Issuing Credit ("It's our policy.")
6. Highest Number of No-Show Service Techs.

TW Cable has also been nominated for a new category, tentatively named "Highest Customer Blood Pressure Count."

FUN WITH MYSPACE

I've never checked out any of these role-playing Internet games like the Sims, but their ubiquity demands acknowledgement, *n'est-ce pas*?

(The Kid From Brooklyn says: For the love o' Mike, fuhgeddabout the friggin' French for cryin' out loud. Ain't plain old English good enough for ya?)

Yeah, like I was sayin':

The increasingly participatory nature of the Internet will only continue to expand, surely.

(Kid: Don't call me Shirley.)

Which is why Napster won't die, why there is a Wikipedia, why the idea of a website Guestbook is only sticking a toe in the water, and why hackers wielding worms and viruses exist in the first place.

Rule #13: The Light exists because of the Dark; there is a little piece of Dark in every Light; pure Light, having been attained, begins to move towards Dark almost immediately. And vice verse all of above–q.v. the yin-yang symbol.

Rule #14: Data exists in order to be manipulated.

Come to find out that MySpace is hosting all manner of role-players who have assumed the cyber identities of a diverse array of deceased individuals (and television characters) including Sarah Vaughan, Ella Fitzgerald, Stan Getz, Mingus, Dvorak, Thelonious Monk, Richard Wagner, King Louis XIV, Kaiser Wilhelm, Rasputin, and Archie Bunker.

To complete the circle (after all, we would not want the Cyberhall of Fame to be entirely self-referential, now would we?) these individuals can be "friended" and therefore linked to the profiles of their living admirers.

The act of "friending" Sarah Vaughan–even though by doing so I guess I would be declaring my profound respect and the great pleasure I receive from her work–ignores the fact that she herself has not been complicit in the "friending" process since she has been dead since 1990 and can no longer click the "accept" button. So I feel that having her photo on my "Friends" page would be rather one-sided, at best.

Unless people are using the word Friend in the sense of "support", like Friends of the East Brunswick Volunteer Ambulance Drivers Association. That I could see.

But the finer points of syntax, connotation, philosophy and even morality fall by the wayside in Cyberspace, because as Mr. McLuhan pointed out so perspicaciously back in 1964, The Medium Is The Message, all by itself.

(Kid: The game's on. Pass the Doritos.)

Terry

GRAND PRIZE

Dunkin Donuts has a scratch-off card they give out with your order. You scratch off one of two boxes to reveal your prize.

I have evidently won a free donut. But what I would really like to win is the Grand Prize of a Toyota FJ Cruiser.

Is there really, somewhere out there in customer land, a scratch-off card that has "Toyota FJ Cruiser" underneath one of the boxes? Somehow, I doubt it.

How would you claim your prize? Go to the counter, order a coffee and say, "Oh by the way, I'd like to claim my Grand Prize," and shove the card over toward the server?

What if you're in a hurry–you really need the new Toyota quickly–can you just go to the drive-in window? (In your old car, of course.)

–What's that, honey?

–It's a Dunkin Donuts scratch-off card game.

–Did you win?

–I dunno. Scratch off a box.

–It says. . . "Toyota FJ Cruiser." Does that mean you win that?

–Yeah, right. Toss it.

Or even better, how about this scenario:

Somewhere, on a sidewalk littered with newspaper and old lottery cards, lies a Dunkin Donuts scratch-off card. One box is scratched off, revealing the words "Sorry, better luck next time."

But underneath the other, unscratched, box–are the words "Toyota FJ Cruiser."

Do you think we can get Guy de Maupassant to flesh this out a little bit? He's probably got a MySpace page . . .

Inside the Mind of a Musician

This reminds me of the time I played Foxwoods with the Lombardo band. Janice was on the gig, and she wanted us to hang out and play the slots. But she only wanted to spend ten dollars. I hate casinos. But to humor her I said okay, but I get to pick which machines we use. She agreed.

My plan was: To psychically ascertain which machine was 9 months pregnant and about to give birth to sextuplets. I soon found it. This machine's aura was fairly quivering with payload.

I directed Janice to the machine and watched incredulously as she put in a one-dollar coin and pulled the handle.

I explained to her that the big payload would only deliver if she put in a three dollar bet, not a one dollar bet.

She then explained to me that the game would be over too quickly if she did that.

So I said, do you want to pull the crank like a schmuck, or do you want to win some money?

To which she replied by ignoring me and continuing to put in another dollar bet, which then paid out some paltry amount, which had she put in the three dollar bet like I said to do, would have yielded a veritable avalanche of silver. But no.

NYC MARATHON

Personally, if I wanted to get from Staten Island to Central Park–I would drive.

The runners pass by, less than a block from my Brooklyn studio. I'm debating whether to go down and check it out. Mainly because Dunkin Donuts is giving away free coffee today. They are right on the race route. Hey, maybe

Terry

I'll even win that Toyota FJ Cruiser–then I'll be able to make that drive from Staten to Manhattan!

The runners' pants
I cannot hear
The runners' pants
I cannot see

and the latter are not to be missed, as they are surely housing some exquisite-looking lower extremities.

I can't see
the race from here
but I can hear it
you see

I cannot hear the panting breaths
nor the plastic thunks
of empty water bottles landing on 4th Avenue.

    What I CAN hear is the kibbitzing of the onlookers, which seems to consist mostly of typical sport-observer Neanderthal-like grunts, cries and shouts, peppered with lots of spicy expletives.

    Not to put down organized sports or anything. After all, we need SOMETHING for the Gammas and Deltas.

    Frankly, it's been so nice in my sunny garden today, that even coffee and skin-tight superhero outfits don't tempt me to leave my house.

    Now that the afternoon is waning and the sun is going behind that big tree, though, I may ditch the backyard and go get my free coffee and my free glimpses of calves, quads and glutes.

LIVE STRONG-EAT YOUR VEGETABLES

–Is that a blue Lance Armstrong "live strong" bracelet on your wrist?

–No. It's a blue rubber band from a head of broccoli from Key Food.

THE COST OF DOING BUSINESS

Recently I was asked to curate a regular jazz night at the Brooklyn Lyceum. For the uninitiated, the word "curate," traditionally used to signify the person who selects the works for an art exhibition, is now being used in music circles. Thus, the term "curator" is basically a fancy name for "the person who books the room."

The idea of curating a regular jazz night is attractive, because one can book one's own bands and the bands of one's friends, and others that are deemed worthy. One becomes a producer in a sense. If one has such aspirations, that can make up for the myriad inconveniences involved in being the booking agent—like phone calls, scheduling, re-scheduling, and acting as go-between twixt the artist and the venue. Having produced many of my own shows, and a few shows for others, I must confess that I consider myself ideally suited to the role.

I turned it down. Here's why:

In my meeting with one of the directors, he explained the financial arrangement: the house gets the first $5 of the ticket price, or 50% of the cover charge, whichever is greater.

Terry

Now, on the rare occasion when I work for "the door" (bringing in nearly 100% of the customers from my own personal mailing list and fan base) I get all the door money. The venue keeps all the food and liquor money. Is this not easy, and fair? And remember, no one would be coming to the place if there weren't a band playing.

In the event that the venue does its own share of advertising (not the usual case, believe me) then any customers who attend as a result of this advertising would, in any case, be coming because of the act appearing there, not because of any intrinsic value in the venue itself.

When I do accept a "door gig," the only one working for the door is me. I do not ask my band members to work for the door. As a bandleader, if need be, I take a loss. You gotta pay the band.

(Reminiscing here about a funny story from Bill Crow's column in Allegro, the Local 802 newspaper. Two men were overheard in conversation: "I owned a jazz club, but it closed. You have to pay the musicians, you know." "Yeah, that's what kills it.")

So the idea of the house taking half of the cover charge for itself simply rubs me the wrong way. Clubs aren't doing this in Europe. They aren't even doing it in California! So how did New York become the Center for Unpaid Bands that club people seem to think it should be?

Musicians—if you must work for the door, get it all, for goodness sake. You brought the audience there, it's your money. "Lose" the gig if they won't agree. But frankly, I feel the loss is theirs, not yours. If you take a door gig for less than 100% of the door, you are losing. Let the sub-standard bands do that if they want. But if you respect yourself and the quality of your performance, then just say no to exploitative deals that do nothing for you but provide a space to play.

Don't listen to their stupid rationale, which goes something like this: "Well, we're providing a space for you to play, with a PA system. We can't afford to pay you, too."

You say: "Yes, you're also providing a refrigerator for all those sodas and beers you sell. Do you get those free? Did P.C. Richards donate the fridge and the coffeemaker? Look, this is the cost of doing business! If you can't afford to pay the acts (whom you're not paying anyway, the customers are paying them with the cover charge) then you can't afford to have a music club. *Capisce?*"

Do what I do. Find a small auditorium in a school or church, or other public space. Find a private loft, art gallery, or dance space where you can put on your show. Rent chairs if you have to, I've done it. Produce the show yourself, or with a partner, or another band. When you do a door gig at a club, you're pretty much producing it yourself anyway.

Let's show these rip-off clubs that we're too good to settle for what they're offering. Let the crappy bands play there. Eventually, some people will notice the difference.

A "MARTHA" DAY

On Friday I went to buy a set of bedsheets. I came home with a 300-thread-count set featuring a pretty, faded-burgundy flower print on a cream background. And because mama didn't raise no fool, I did NOT pay retail.

You can do the same if you head down to 86th Street in Bay Ridge, Brooklyn, where the Century 21 department store presides over two city blocks. Allow three hours to find a parking spot.

Terry

It occurred to me today to analyze the print pattern on the sheets. Even though it is busy, it's a restful pattern on the eyes, and this is not just because of the mellow colors.

If the pattern were polka dots, say, it would drive me crazy–all the dots being the same size.

But the print has three different flower groupings; let's call them A, B, C.

The pattern only makes sense if you look at the flow of it in one direction–then you can see a linear pattern of A, B, C that is either vertical or horizontal depending on whether you're looking at a sheet or a pillowcase.

It's kind of like the vertical lines of code in The Matrix computer screen.

The adjacent pattern line is placed so that A is aligned between B and C of the line next to it, and so on.

So the pattern simulates randomness (like snowflakes, raindrops, clouds, etc.) while closer inspection, Dr. Watson, reveals its underlying pattern.

My "eureka" moment so excited me that I rushed to phone up the head of the Nobel committee. But he/she must have died, because he/she is not returning my calls.

In a true "graphic design imitates life" moment, I rejected the matching quilt cover and purchased a staid brown with subtle squares. Too much chaos–no matter the underlying pattern–can't be a good thing.

SUMMER IN THE CITY

Brooklyn: it's summer again, (ok, Spring, close enough) and you know what THAT means. . . Mr. Softee and his trucks descend on our communities, purveying products to harm our health, all to a very loud tune.

According to the Environmental Protection Agency, as of July 2007 the trucks have been prohibited from playing their loudspeaker jingle while stationary.

Who knew?

Evidently not the ice cream guys, because they are still playing it at top volume, dishing out decibels, dessert and carbon monoxide to the whole neighborhood.

The guy who was just outside (at 10:15 p.m., mind you!) had the speaker volume so high that EVEN THE KIDS COMPLAINED! Given the volume that kids are used to, this is a clear indication that I am not just an old fogey with an acoustic axe to grind.

Of course, when I go up to the window and complain, they are always really polite and they turn it down right away. But why should I have to go out there three times a day?

Anyway, now that I know what the law is, I PLAN TO DESTROY THE MR. SOFTEE CARTEL.

Let me take this opportunity to encourage all of you to join the mission, which I am dubbing OPERATION 6/8. Jot down the plate number of the truck and the time, and dial 311. Mr. Softee's assault on our hearing and peace of mind must be stopped!

ROBERT'S BIKE TRIP

My friend Robert finished a 4,200 mile cross country bike tour that started at the Pacific Ocean in Oregon, and ended today at the Atlantic Ocean at Coney Island. He did it alone, camping out at night and riding during the day.

He looks great–kind of like Tom Hanks in Castaway after he'd been on the desert island for four years–but with less hair.

Terry

On hand to greet him were some of us taiji people and some family members, sporting Sandy's decorated T shirts. Spider and Fury did their own though. Spider's had some interesting creatures on the front. I guessed lobster, alligator, praying mantis, dragon, and I was wrong till I got to dinosaur.

It was a gorgeous day and there were a fair amount of folks on the beach, including two guys who were building what appeared to be an extremely elaborate sand castle, using industrial-looking containers and shovels. I could be wrong though–it's possible they were breaking ground on the next Russian condominium complex.

A lot of people came up to Robert, whose bicycle was outfitted with saddle bags and other accoutrements, and asked him where he biked from. I rather think they were expecting an answer like "New Jersey," not "Oregon."

A number of questions were posed, including at least one query as to the state of his mental health. "Are you crazy?" the lady said.

According to Robert, no visit to Coney Island is complete without a ride on the Cyclone, the legendary wooden roller coaster that will battle you for your lunch.

My comment: I've belayed off of cliffs, gone white water canoeing, back country skiing across frozen rivers, jumped out of an airplane, walked across hot coals. . . but I ain't ridin' on THAT thing!

HAUNTED APARTMENT?

Getting a new pull chain put in a ceiling fan, I got into a conversation with the fan guy.

It seems that one of his customers bought a remote control for her ceiling fan/light combo. But as soon as she installed it, her lights started going on and off by themselves, at random. She complained.

At the same time, her upstairs neighbor, who had just moved in, was experiencing the same problem. They met up in the elevator.

"How do you like the apartment?" she asked. The neighbor replied that he liked it fine, except he was moving out, because it was haunted! It seems that the apartment had become available because of the death of the previous tenant, an elderly lady. She died in the apartment.

Evidently the lady's ghost was haunting the apartment, said the neighbor, because the lights kept going on and off by themselves!

The woman explained that it wasn't necessary for the neighbor to move out, as the ceiling fan guy was coming the next day to reprogram her fan's RFID chip to a different frequency than the neighbor's.

BEN FRANKLIN'S LEGACY

Will someone please explain to me why, when I go to Fairway in Red Hook and pay for my groceries with a hundred dollar bill, the cashier screams "BILL CHECK!" more times than seems necessary, and the manager has to come running over, and my poor little Ben Franklin is put through the most embarrassing public examination before being inserted into the cashier's drawers. I mean drawer.

Conversely, I go to the check cashing place on 4th Ave. and shove a bunch of Bens under the window, and they are accepted without question and a money order is immediately dispensed.

Any elucidation on the above will be much appreciated.

Terry

SUPER PLUMBER

After the second toilet stopped flushing, we knew it was a job for . . . SUPER PLUMBER!

With shaking finger we perused the Brooklyn Yellow Book, searching desperately for help.

Seduced by a full-page ad promising quick rescue, and featuring a photo of a gleaming truck, we dialed the number.

Help would be on the way within the hour, we were promised. Gil went to use the bathroom at Dunkin Donuts. I manned the fort, mop and towels at the ready.

After an hour we got the call: "Where do you live again?"

Help was on the way.

I answered the door, expecting Super Plumber with– if not a cape–then holstered plunger, pipe wrench and superhero plumber aplomb.

I got two oafs in a white van who didn't wipe their feet when they came in.

Yes, perhaps it was naive of me, after reading the ad that boasted of conquests over sewer lines, leaky pipes, obstreperous boilers and Aegean Stables maintenance, to believe in chivalrous sewer saviors in shiny trucks–but I can dream, can't I?

MY ANNUAL DAY AT THE BEACH

This year, no one came up to me offering a 10 lb. striped bass. Sorry, Elysa.

I was, however, perhaps one of the first to witness a new sport called "kite-boarding." Maybe this has been around for years, but I've never seen it. These two guys had huge kites that looked almost like modern parachutes (NOT those round ones from WW II), and they wore harnesses with the kite cables strapped to them. On the sand, it looked like they could easily go airborne. Then one of the guys got in the water with the kite, and a very small surfboard with foot straps. He then proceeded to mount the board and sail around on the water–it was way cool. Earlier, the lifeguard patrol had stopped some other guys from surfing too far away. Then the police stopped in front of where this guy was kite-boarding, but they drove on so I guess they were just watching.

I know it's called kite-boarding because I asked the guy later. Then he asked me what I was doing with the ball. "Sphereplay," I told him.

Sphereplay is my new thing. You roll the sphere across your hands and body in such a way as to make it look like the ball is sticking to you. I bought a 3" diameter acrylic sphere at the Zhang San Feng Festival, and took a class in how to do it. Today I discovered it is really fun to play with the sphere at the beach, because dry sand doesn't stick to it (you drop the sphere quite often, especially when you're learning a new trick.)

People come up and ask what it is because it looks so cool. When I was a kid, I really wanted to be cool. Now that I finally AM cool, I don't give a rat's ass. (Oh my God, a jock is talking to me!)

Terry

THE EAGLE FLIES ON FRIDAY

THE EAGLE FLIES ON FRIDAY

The job last night was a birthday party for some REALLY rich people in Alpine, NJ. It was just me and Jonathan Hanser, so it was a lot of playing. The agent pitched it as a jazz gig, but it turns out the client wanted SMOOTH Jazz. Bummer. Because anyone that requests Smooth Jazz is sure to be a loser. And they were. Their friends were losers too.

The ironic part of it is, I'm sure that people with a 10 million dollar house don't think of themselves as losers. But they are.

Be comforted: F U R RDNG THS, U R NT A LSR.

Or if you are, there's still hope for you, because you're reading this book.

Today's realization: THE WHOLE WORLD IS A CLUB DATE. That's so empowering. Once you realize that, you can do anything.

PENSION PACKAGE PERKS

How many of us take a job for the perks?

I submit that money is good for the body, but Perks Are Good For The Soul. If you are not getting Adequate Perks, you should quit your job right now.

Of course, one person's perk can be another's poison. Or to put it differently: a perk in Portland might not be worth a bialy in Brooklyn.

[Perhaps Paul Simon is available to set the above paragraph to music, because I can't be bothered.]

Terry

In any event, all this is just the preamble to a perk that I would like to pring to your pretention:

On my wall is a framed letter from Bill Clinton (it did not come in a frame–it came in the mail–the frame is from Staples) in which he thanks me for sending him a copy of my practice book, which by the way I sent to him because he really needs it. But I'm sure he's very busy with other things and doesn't have much time for the horn. Though it would be really good if he were on Oprah or something, and she happened to say something like "So Bill (if she calls him 'Bill'–I don't really know), what have you been up to lately?" and then he would say something like "I've been practicing my saxophone a lot. Here's a practice book I've been using [and here he holds up a copy of my book for the camera to get a close up of] and it's really been helping me" and then Oprah could say, "Well let's hear how much you've improved since you've been using Su Terry's book Practice Like The Pros" and then Mr. Clinton could whip out his sax and sit in with the band (oh wait, I don't think Oprah has a band, better make that the Letterman Show–please go back and change 'Oprah' to 'Dave') and gosh darn it if he doesn't sound pretty good!

My my, what a tangent we've gone off on. This stream-of-consciousness blogging style can be dangerous...

Back to the note. The note says [this part is real, no fooling now]: "Dear Su, Thank you so much for the copy of your saxophone practice book Practice Like The Pros. You were kind to remember my love of the saxophone, and I appreciate your thoughtfulness. All the best to you. Sincerely, Bill Clinton."

It's a personal, typed letter. I was glad to receive it. I think Bill Clinton is one of the most intelligent persons ever to have occupied the White House, and he was certainly a great President for jazz.

But let's get right to the perk.

I saved the envelope, and the envelope has in the top right hand corner a facsimile of Mr. Clinton's signature, and below it the words "Postage and Fees Paid."

Now, I think that is a pretty darn good perk, never having to buy stamps again for THE REST OF YOUR LIFE.

I would even venture to say that the small pleasure I receive from waiting in line at the post office to buy and use some cute stamps, like the Gee's Bend Quilt ones that I just got, is easily mitigated, if not heavily outweighed, by the perk offered by Our Lady of Perpetual Postage.

I petter put a pop to piss pefore pie pet in pubble.

CECI N'EST PAS UN CHEQUE

We got a nice Christmas check in the mail the other day for $40,000.00 That's forty thousand dollars and no cents. It seems that in order to cash this check, we would have to sign some papers or something that had to do with our house. Seemed like a lot of bother for a measly forty thou. Oh, and also on the front of the check in small letters, about a 6 pt. font I believe, were the words 'This is not a check.'

Rene Magritte, the Surrealist painter extraordinaire, were he living today, would undoubtedly glow with pride at this modern-day appropriation of one of his most famous works–"Ceci N'est Pas Une Pipe," or 'This Is Not A Pipe." It is a painting of a pipe.

Likewise, our $40,000 check is not a check. It is only a picture of a check. And this, my friends, surely proves that the Surrealists were right all along!

Terry

GRAMMY AWARDS

I just got my invitation to the 48th Annual Grammy Awards, and thought you all might like to know how much the tickets cost.

For Pre-Telecast and Telecast seating only: Platinum is for VIP loge-level seating, $900. Member Gold, loge-level, $350. Member Silver, mid-level seating, $225. Member Bronze, upper-level, $125. But if you want to go to the Grammy Celebration Party also, you've got to fork over another $200. Or you can just go to the party. It's Feb. 8. It's in L.A. I'm not going.

But if Gilly's Caper gets nominated next year, hell, I'll be there. Unless I get a gig.

HELLO, YOU'RE SUPPOSED TO GET PAID FOR THIS

Yet another rip-off scam feeding off musicians: An advertisement on MySpace urges bands to submit a song for a chance to be chosen for the television show Supernatural.

"Music has always been the heart and soul of this show." –Eric Kripke, Executive Producer

Hello, excuse me, Mr. Kripke. I'm so glad that, as you state, "music [is] the heart and soul of this show." That being the case, you must have enormous respect for the folks who create the music–or am I wrong? Are you aware that music for television and film is often a major part of the income of a composer? Are you aware that a Synchronization License is normally procured for such a broadcast, and that the composer is normally paid a fee for the use of the music? Oh yes, I'm sure you are. And isn't it wonderful to not have to pay these fees? Of course by bypassing the usual channels (which exist so that composers can make a living) you can be proud of having gotten a bargain by ripping off those very musicians whose music is, as you say, "the heart and soul of this show." Yes, I imagine you will score a few brownie points with your boss for that one.

MUSICIANS: You are in business, don't forget that. Your music is valuable. If you offer a track or two as a freebie on your website, fine. But DON'T give away your music to a network TV show. This show airs internationally and the first season was produced by Warner Bros. According to Wikipedia, THERE ARE NO CREDITS aired, so what good would it do you to have your music on there anyway–no one would know you wrote it. Please use some common sense and be circumspect about whom you give your music to for free.

Check out the "Official Rules," which state: "Grand Prize has no retail value." This is a lie. Music for television does have a retail value, as does music for film. If you "won" this "contest", you would have to sign a release for them to use your music. If your music had no retail value, then why would you have to sign a release? I can't go into any more detail in this forum, but if you don't understand what I'm saying, please refer to some books on the music business. There are many.

JACKIE O

Last night I opened for Andrea Reese in "Cirque Jacqueline" at the Triad Theater in NYC, which is a fantastic one woman play if you get a chance to catch it. Not being a follower of Jackie O, Princess Di, or any of their ilk, I knew very little about Jackie's life. She had the bearing of a princess, but was very warm and funny as well.

Margot Leverett was there to watch the show (she was the one who recommended me to Andrea) and we went out afterwards for sushi. The waiter brought me some vile tasting cold sake, so I decided to steal some of Jackie's act: I called the manager over and told him the sake was not acceptable. He went into standard weasel mode. I leaned on the table and just looked at him. He repeated his spiel, word for word. I just smiled, moved the glass gently toward him, and said softly, "Please, take it away."

We got the bill afterwards, sans sake.

THE END OF PROFESSIONAL MUSICIANS, 2ND INSTALLMENT

A chick on MySpace e mails me, and presumably all the other New York musicians on MySpace, to say she's booking a club downtown, am I interested. I ask for more information. This is an excerpt from her response:

"Sets are ½hour to 45mins. Depending on your draw. Load-in time is an hour before your set. Our shows work as follows; Admission for 21 and over $8 @ the door. Cover for Friday and Saturday is $10 for 21+. We do insist that all bands performing with us have a following. We do help build fan base at your request. Starting at 10 people paid at the door to see your show, your band will receive 25%; if there are 25 people then the band receives 30%. Bands will get 40% of 40 + fans.

**We do have a 10-person minimum. If a band brings less than 10 people they will not be paid for the show.

Inside the Mind of a Musician

**Once you make your 10-person minimum we will give you 2 drink tickets per band member for every 10 people that you draw. If your band has a good turn out we will offer you additional concerts.
Note This is a must***
All bands/performers must list their shows with Bend Over Productions [name changed to avoid giving these schmucks free advertising] on MYSPACE.
Also they must give a credit to Bend Over Productions.

Filming & Editing Service with East Bend Films: Bend Over Productions is now offering filming and editing services for live performances. Bend Over Productions provides a professional camera and camera operator to capture your performance and uses top of the line editing systems to create a professional product. Together, we will make your live event forever memorable with a one-of-a-kind video. Any performer or band that brings more than 40 fans to a show will receive a free video. Bend Over Productions offers a discount to any performers performing at a Bend Over Productions event. If you are interested in Bend Over Productions filming and editing services, please visit our website.
Thanks!
Ashley"

Well, Ashley, let's go through this point by point: Number one, my set is only a half hour to 45 minutes so you can cram in as many bands as possible in one night.

You're relying on my personal mailing list to bring in customers for your club so you can keep 60 to 75% of the cover charges that MY PEOPLE have paid to SEE ME AND MY BAND.

Terry

Since you don't say you're giving me a percentage of the drinks that you sell, I assume that you keep all of that money. Now, that's not very nice! I share with you, but you won't share with me? OH I FORGOT, you're providing the venue! According to your description, "a candlelit dive bar in Chinatown." Yes, that should make a great backdrop for the VIDEO that you will make of my performance that you kindly offered to SELL TO ME, or if I bring in enough fans (whose cover charges mostly go to you, not to mention your profit on drinks), I will get for free. "Free" being a relative term.

Not to mention the unsavory possibility that, should I become even more famous than I already am, five years from now I will get calls from my friends saying "I just saw you on TV in some candlelit dive bar in Chinatown! What a pit! I hope you got paid!"

Plus everyone in my band gets two free drink tickets! Wow! (For every ten people we draw, that is.)

I especially like this line:

"Together, we will make your live event forever memorable with a one-of-a-kind video."

What is this, my bat mitzvah?

And also I have to give your production company free advertising in all my publicity–publicity that I pay for myself, both in postage and time?

I think we've covered the main points. If I weren't having so much fun busting you, Ashley girl, then your e mail wouldn't even be worth a reply.

All this is further proof of my conjecture that the music industry is booking amateurs because they don't have to pay them.

The sad part is that evidently the audience can't tell the difference, or even worse, they can tell the difference but they don't care. It's the whole "American Idol" syndrome, where they throw the amateurs to the lions. Now, that's entertainment! And yes, the reference to the ancient Roman Colosseum is intentional.

I can't speak for other types of music, but I know that in jazz music, the player's game has to be up at all times. If you're not playing the music constantly, you lose your edge. That's why players do things that don't pay, like rehearsal bands and GIGS THAT PAY NOTHING OR NEXT TO IT, because you've got to keep your chops up.

It's a shame that schools are turning out excellent young musicians by the thousands who will not be able to make a living by performing. But many of them will make excellent teachers, who can, in turn, train thousands more to not make a living.

I guess as long as audiences are more entertained by mistakes and inexperience than by seasoned performers, then the trend will continue.

Personally, I don't attend a performance to see someone fail. That is not entertaining to me.

But that "glass half full" part of me can't help thinking that many folks would choose experienced, professional performers if they could.

Unfortunately, the choices are largely controlled by an industry that wants to make the highest possible profit, regardless of the quality of the "product." Evidently, a large segment of the music/entertainment industry will not give consumers the choices they deserve.

HOW TO MILK A PER DIEM

I just played up at Mohegan Sun, the resort/casino in Uncasville, Connecticut, with the Tony Danza Show. The show is a total blast! The band is great (Lenny LaCroix, John Arbo, Dave Shoup, Eddie Caccavale and me) and Tony has a very nice voice and does some great tap dancing numbers, mostly on standards. We open at Feinstein's in New York tomorrow night, for two weeks, for you locals.

But about the PD: Mohegan Sun gives you a $50 food credit that's good in most of their restaurants. In addition, you get a pass to eat in the employee cafeteria, which has very good food.

I was thinking, why do I need to eat in the cafeteria if I have a $50 food credit in the restaurants? Then I figured out the strategy: you eat in the cafeteria for free during the day. Then after the show, at one of the upscale restaurants, you have a $30 single malt and a goat cheese salad or something, and you're good! Eddie has it down to a science– I saw a couple of his checks. $49.57, $49.08. I can learn from him.

ANYONE WANT TO BUY A BRIDGE?

I often speak about the various unpredictable situations that occur to performers. One just happened.

I sent a newspaper reporter a digital photo–as is customary–to accompany her article on me. In the online version of the article, the newspaper is offering PRINTS OF THE PHOTO FOR SALE!

Choice of sizes, you can even buy it framed!

I was completely floored by this blatant abuse of the photo.

Obviously the reproduction rights to the photo belong not to the newspaper, but to the photographer. In this case, the photographer happens to be a highly regarded professional with an international reputation. She makes her living as a photographer. Although both legally and morally, that is beside the point.

Even though I'm careful to always include the photo credit with digital pics, I now see that I will have to add a sentence stipulating that the usage permission pertains only to reproduction in the newspaper or website, not to the SALE of reproductions.

Next thing you know, the newspaper will be selling mp3 downloads of files that artists sent to reporters who were interviewing them. It's the same thing, is it not?

Only I think the RIAA would not allow that to happen, or it would have happened already.

That's what the photography community needs, a good pitbull like the RIAA.

I wrote to the reporter and asked her whom I should contact about this issue. I'll let you know the outcome of this bizarre scenario.

UPDATE ON PHOTO SCENARIO

They fixed it! (See previous entry)

The photo editor explained in an e mail to me that it is an automated process with all photos that accompany articles.

Somehow I doubt that all their online photos are supplied by their staff photographers. Moral(s) of the story:
A) I still have to add a "Use Notice" to jpegs I send out.
B) Freelance photographers beware.
C) The Internet eats everything in its path.

"It's an automated process"–wasn't that one of the defenses presented at the Nuremberg Trials?

Terry

WHO LIKES WHOM?

You may think, judging from the title of this post, that I'm about to indulge in idle (is there any other kind?) gossip. Heavens, nothing could be further from the truth.

I want to share with you an interesting website I found called www.opensecrets.org. There you can see where the presidential candidates are getting their contributions from.

Evidently contributions of $500 or more are tallied by their PAC affiliations, as well as members, employees and owners of organizations. So here's the beef:

McCain's top contributors are affiliated with Merrill Lynch, Citigroup, Blank Rome LLP, Greenberg Traurig LLP, and AT&T. In other words, mostly finance folks.

Obama's top contributors are affiliated with Goldman Sachs, Univ. of California, JP Morgan Chase, UBS AG, and Citigroup. Others include Univ. of Chicago and Harvard. In other words, finance and higher education.

Ron Paul's top contributors are affiliated with the U.S. Army, Google, U.S. Air Force, Microsoft, U.S. Navy, U.S. Post Office. Others include IBM, Intel, Apple, Boeing and Hewlett Packard. In other words, the military and the computer industry.

And what conclusions can we draw from this revelation? Hell if I know.

YOU WON! NOW GIVE US YOUR SONG FOR FREE

In yet another scam victimizing young musicians and composers, the TV show "90210" is trolling the talent pool for unsuspecting newbies in search of their big break.

A common scam these days is to hold a "contest" for the best theme song, the "prize" being the use of your song on the show.

Yes, you heard right. The winner of this contest gets to give away their song to the show in question, relinquishing the fees and royalties he/she is supposed to be paid.

While this particular "contest" asks for a cover version of their regular theme, many others want an original theme.

But who wouldn't want to give away their music to a major TV network (in this case, CBS) for the chance to be heard by millions? Isn't that worth a lot of money? Yeah, it is. THAT'S WHY YOU'RE SUPPOSED TO GET PAID FOR IT.

How about the actors on the show? Do they get paid, or are they so grateful to be on TV that they waive that little detail? Besides, don't they get free food on the set?

How about the camera people, wardrobe staff, makeup dept., catering team? I'm sure they are so thrilled to be involved with a major production that they donate their time. Besides, don't they get free food AND coffee on the set?

Please, young musicians and composers–join a union (AFM, AFTRA) and a performing rights organization (BMI, ASCAP, SESAC) and learn the business, because this is a business. Do not give away your services to those who can and do pay for them. You are entitled to be paid for your music and your performances–don't let anyone tell you otherwise.

There are also a number of trade organizations such as the Songwriters Guild of America (www.songwritersguild.com) who host events and whose

Terry

members do get the types of gigs you would like to have someday. These people are a wealth of information and will be happy to share their knowledge with you.

STILL THE SAME OLD BIZ

If you watch old movies about musicians, you can see that nothing about the music business has changed.

In Humoresque, John Garfield plays a young violinist trying to break into the business. Oscar Levant plays his accompanist buddy, and he tells him either he has to fork over about $750 (my, times HAVE changed!) for hall rental, publicity and a decent violin, or else find a wealthy patron who will do the same. So even then, talent wasn't enough. Ya gotta have dough too.

There's a film about George Sand and Chopin and Liszt called, I think, Interludes. There's a scene in the movie where they are all on a picnic, and Liszt mentions that he's going to play a benefit to help the victims of a famine, and his wife goes ballistic that he's going to play for free when they need money so badly.

In a more modern film–a documentary about Madonna–there's a scene where she's onstage during the tech rehearsal, screaming at the sound man.

I saw that and I was like, wow–even MADONNA'S sound man screws up! Nobody is immune to the vagaries of human error, no matter how high up they are!

I don't know, somehow it's comforting to know that the crap we deal with today is the same crap that we've always dealt with. It gives one sort of a warm, fuzzy, HISTORICAL feeling. Or is it hysterical? I guess that's why most musicians have a highly developed sense of humor–you gotta laugh to keep from crying!

INSURANCE UPDATE

Just to let you know the progress we're not making on getting the insurance company to make good on our two televisions and three other devices that got zapped in the big lightning storm three weeks ago–

Their instructions on making the claim were as follows:

1. Kill the Medusa and bring back the head.
2. Clean out the Aegean Stables.
3. Have your repairperson (here I take the liberty of modernizing their antiquated terminology) fill out the enclosed five affidavits with the complete information on each item and the estimated cost of repair. Mail these back to us, then maybe we can talk. Maybe.

YOU CAN'T AUTOGRAPH A DOWNLOAD

Do you know what band has sold the most albums and CDs ever?

Take a guess.

The Beatles? Nope.

The Rolling Stones? Nope.

Charlie Parker and the Parakeets? Nope. (OK I made that one up.)

No, the winner of the Most Units Sold contest is a heavy metal band called AC/DC. You cannot go to iTunes and buy their albums   You cannot stream them on Rhapsody.

The point being that AC/DC never bought into the whole download thing (until 2012, when they released their catalogue to iTunes–ed.) Back in the fairly recent day when every music pundit from here to Antarctica was saying that musicians simply HAD to be in the Great Download Game by licensing their music to one or more of the prevailing Internet music sites, AC/DC just said no.

And look where they are today. They are on top.

Everyone else is, if not on the bottom, then at least a rung below. Even if they are a cut above.

I intend to make most, if not all, of my future albums as digital downloads. Mainly because I'm tired of storing boxes of CDs in my house. As entropy rolls down the pike in a head-on-collision trajectory, I need to regain control of my closets!

JAZZ BIZ

Gene Solon sent me a copy of Marty Khan's book "Straight Ahead–A Comprehensive Guide to the Business of Jazz." I started reading it and was impressed with Marty's ability to "re-frame" the situation.

Re-framing is an idea touted by the legendary psychotherapist and hypnotist Milton Erickson; today, I suppose one might need a Spin Doctor rather than a psychotherapist. Nevertheless, the exact same powers can be used for good or for evil, as we well know.

Marty discusses how the jazz business is built on the "failure" model, whereby the industry makes more money when projects are in their beginning, "failure" stage, rather than in their later "successful" stage in which more profit goes to the artist rather than the company. He points out that expenses on a recording are all recoupable, meaning that the artist makes no royalties whatsoever until all the expenses have been paid off. So in fact, the recording company (which frequently is part of a mega-corporation that also owns the manufacturing plant, the distribution company, etc.) actually breaks even after only a few thousand records have been sold, rather than the 20,000 unit figure that is in the artist's contract.

That's why I have my own company–so I can lose ALL the money, instead of just a percentage.

So anyway, we could go on about this for days. But I just like the way he puts things in perspective–because obviously there's a lot of money to be made in jazz, even though its popularity may not equal that of pop music. He quotes funk recording artist/performer George Clinton to make his point: "the drug problem will never be solved because there's more money in the business of FIGHTING drugs than there is in the business of SELLING drugs."

Hey, it's almost enough to send you off the grid! One could go live with the Amish, for example. The food at the Amish Market that was downtown before 9/11 was really good. . .

But I can't go live off the grid yet, because I have to finish this song I'm writing called "I'm Buyin' You A One-Way Ticket To Pluto."

After that, maybe.

WHOSE LAW

Everyone is familiar with "Murphy's Law", which says that anything that can go wrong, will go wrong. Does anyone know the name of the law that states "The degree of enjoyment of the gig will be in inverse proportion to the amount it pays."?

Terry

TOUGH BUSINESS

Regarding the jazz biz, or the music biz, Gandalfe writes "seems like a tough business for a woman."

You know, I have to say it's a tough business, period! When I was younger, and I'd hear about a player who quit the business, I'd be amazed. How could anyone quit??? But then the older I got, the more I understood it. By this time, I know many people who have left the music business. I also think about some of the really great players who left New York and went back to their hometowns, and did who knows what?

The fact is, there are only a few ways to be financially successful in this work:

1. Be in a high-profile touring band. My friend Tim Ries plays with the Rolling Stones and has done many tours with them. But as I understand, HE DOES NOT SOLO WITH THEM! This is unbelievable to me, that a great soloist like Tim Ries doesn't get solos with the Stones. WHAT A WASTE!!!

2. Teach music in a school or privately.

3. Broadway. When I first moved to New York in the eighties, the pits were full of not-that-great players who were hip to the nice fat pension contributions that the AFM managed to negotiate way back when. Now, the pits are full of great jazz players, so the quality is much better. Unfortunately, many people can't tell the difference between a live band and Memorex. Charli Persip always says, the downfall of musicians was when they allowed themselves to be removed from the stage where they could be seen as part of the show. "Terrific–now I don't have to wear a tuxedo!" Then they moved pit orchestras into separate rooms, where they accompanied the show via closed circuit TV. "Yeah!

Inside the Mind of a Musician

Now I can wear jeans and T shirts to work!" Note to all musicians: YOU ARE IN THE ENTERTAINMENT BUSINESS, LIKE IT OR NOT.

Now, what number am I on? Oh yeah–

4. Jazz Education. A thriving field. So many great young players hungry for knowledge. There ought to be work for them. . . but there really isn't. Hopefully this will change.

5. Club dates. I really respect the rhythm section players that I do weddings and parties with, they are truly amazing. They know repertoire from the 1920's to the present, and can play practically any style-and do it well.

I'm reminded of the old Chinese curse, "May you live in interesting times." Time will tell how the music unfolds, along with everything else.

When I was around 16, I studied piano with Gay Mehegan. I studied with John Mehegan too, but Gay told me something I'll never forget. One day I was complaining to her that some kids at school picked Timmy to be in their band instead of me. She said, "Listen. In ten years, Timmy won't even be playing the saxophone, AND YOU WILL!" And lo, it came to pass.

Meanwhile, I'm keeping an ear out for the offspring of my musician friends. There's something going on in the kid generation, talent-wise. This may be the generation that establishes the new frontier for creative music. I hope so, because I think the world's ears are ready for a deeper relationship with music–thus necessitating deep music.

Terry

OIL, OR LACK THEREOF

It just doesn't make sense to me how the earth's crust can still be okay after taking the oil out of it. If you did that to a pie crust. . .

Perhaps this is the true meaning of Don McLean's song "Bye Bye Miss American Pie." You know, "took my Chevy to the levee but the levee was dry." A little insider info: After the song became a hit, someone once asked Don McLean what it meant. He said, "it means I only have to work if I want to."

Inside the Mind of a Musician

THE LYRICS OF LIFE

Terry

THE LYRICS OF LIFE

In the bottom of my Qi Note Records messenger bag, which accompanies me on all flights and various other missions, I found a piece of paper on which I had written the following:

"A prophet is never welcomed."

"The only thing that can travel at the speed of light is a massless particle."

"photon, graviton, gluon (strong force particle)"

"If the massless particles leave the emptiness of a vacuum and begin to interact with matter, even they can't travel at the speed of light anymore."

Below this I had the address of a promoter in Florida who, I understand, is no longer promoting. Which proves my theory that if you wait long enough, you don't have to do most of the things you think you have to do, like contact promoters.

As for those other snippets of wisdom, though I wish I could take credit for them, I suspect they were copied from somewhere. The appalling lack of footnotes (to which I am ordinarily attentive) will surely haunt me as I say to someone "A prophet is never welcomed" and they say "That's MY line!"

DRUGS

A young student asked me if I used drugs when I was his age. I told him no, I didn't have to. The guys who wrote Mad Magazine did the drugs, and I just read the magazine.

PURPOSE IN LIFE

Sometimes I like to flatter myself by thinking I was put on earth to play the saxophone.

I was just brushing one of my two cats, and a voice whispered in my ear: "You were put on this earth in order to care for these creatures. Brush them, feed them, stroke them, clean up after them, and love them."

Is this true? Well, my cats act like it is.

A JOURNEY TO INFINITY BEGINS WITH A SINGLE STEP

The concerns of humans are, for the most part, pretty depressing. On the other hand, I have never become depressed while gazing at Nature: seeing trees, hearing the rain, smelling the air and earth, tasting a radish, or touching the silky petals of a rose.

Whenever I think about all the stupid and irrelevant things that humans are evidently compelled to do, I want to kill myself, because being a human, I am compelled to do them also.

Going to work. Watching TV. Shopping. How about enslaving and torturing other creatures, including fellow humans. Truly the zenith of pointlessness.

Did God add Man to the Mix so there would be someone to appreciate His efforts? If so, I think it backfired. Most of the time, we've got zero appreciation, and the planet would be in better shape without us.

Terry

If everything on Earth has a function in the care and feeding of the planet, I can't think what ours would be. And yet, we are still here. There must be a reason. But whatever this reason, this function, may be–its very nature means it is an indelible part of us. It is a layer so deep that not the mind, the body nor the emotions can penetrate it. They can't reach down far enough. This deepest layer, however, being so much a part of our human fabric– indeed its very woof and warp–can occasionally creep into mind, body and emotions and influence them in various ways.

Perhaps our most common connection with the Essential Layer is through our dreams, when mind, body and emotions act out scenarios so unlike those in daily waking life.

Certain other activities–like immersing oneself in great music–can connect one to the Sublime. And this, to me, is the function of art: if it doesn't connect to the Sublime, it's not art. If its essence doesn't reach all the way to Infinity, it's not art. It doesn't have to be Michelangelo either. I've glimpsed Infinity in a handmade quilt. I've heard it in the music of Miles Davis. (Sometimes I think I smell it, after I do a wash with Downy fabric softener, but I'm not sure.)

I'd like to go to the Botanic Garden today, but it's freezing out. So I guess I'll just put a reed on this clarinet and play the blues.

LONELINESS

The other day I was attending a taiji event which took place in a school gym. I got there early and went into the building to wait.

Inside the Mind of a Musician

After having a nice conversation with the maintenance guy, I noticed a parakeet in a cage in an adjacent office.

The parakeet was grooming a smaller bird. The lights were on and the door was ajar, so I went in to take a closer look.

The parakeet was so intent on grooming the other bird that it didn't notice me right away. Then it hopped over to another perch, and I was stunned to see that the smaller bird was made of rubber!

It reminded me of Tom Hanks in Castaway, where he's marooned on a deserted island for years. He paints a face on a washed-ashore soccer ball with blood. He calls it "Wilson," for indeed, that is its name.

Sometimes you just need someone to talk to. And if you say the wrong thing, well, at least she doesn't get her feathers ruffled.

LAWRENCE FERLINGHETTI

I love what he said in his New York Times Sunday Magazine interview:

"The literarians in the world, and there are millions of them. . . are not considered the dominant culture in this country. What's called the dominant culture will fade away as soon as the electricity goes off. In the 60's, there was a famous slogan, 'Be Here Now,' which in fact was a bestselling book by Ram Dass. Today, with the cellphones, the fax, the Internet, the whole schmear–the slogan you have is 'Be Somewhere Else Now.' "

SECRETS

I seem to be the type of person in whom others like to confide. Total strangers come up to me and tell me intimate details about their lives. So I hope none of my friends are getting nervous that I would divulge any confidences in this forum. Like my friend Jim: he said, "Hey Su, that stuff I told you last night, you're not going to put that in your blog, are you?"

"Are you kidding?" I said. "I would never put that in my blog. No way," I assured him. "I'm saving it for my novel!"

"SHEESH"

Yes Deb, the word "sheesh" has indeed crept into my blog. I believe it's the first time I have ever used it [see entry "Tonight's Gig" in OSAMA HATES JAZZ] either in writing or in conversation. Isn't it a great word?

I ONLY USE MY POWERS FOR GOOD

There have always, since time immemorial, existed people who sensed the magical properties of the Universe and attempted to perceive or even to display them. (To display something, all you do is put a 'frame' around it.)

Also there have always existed, in far greater number (or far louder voice), those who wished to refute these properties and persecute the ones who spoke of them.

CARS OF THE STARS

This is my idea for a new magazine. It's along the order of Architectural Digest, but instead of profiling the homes of celebrities, it will feature their cars.

We've all heard about Leonardo diCaprio's Prius, but how many know what color it is? I sure don't. And how about Arnold's Hummer? Inquiring minds want to know–what's in his glovebox? C'mon, I want to see those reporters get down n' dirty under those celebmobiles. I'm dying to know. . . does Keanu Reeves use. . . regular or super?

We learned in physics class that cars are singularities that can retain infinite amounts of any substance that enters their interior. So who cleans up the interior of a celebmobile? Do they have, like, servants for that?

SERIOUSLY, THE JOKE IS DEAD

To the Editor:

While comedians and party-goers have evidently forsaken The Joke, I can assure you it thrives in the fecund environment of Musicians On a Break. When we're sitting around a table in the back room with fifteen minutes to call our own , there's nothing we like better than a good joke. Except maybe a good single malt scotch.

Perhaps it's the stress of playing in a different place every job, or contending with the demands of club owners, clients and bandleaders, but if you were a fly on the wall in a musicians' dressing room, you'd be laughing your proboscis off. We only laugh to keep from crying, mind you. But despite our musicians' sensitivity, no ethnic group, political party or gender goes unscathed in a musician's joke repertoire.

No, The Joke is not dead–it's just on a break.

Terry

PAM'S PARTY

Last night was Pamela's annual Christmas party. I started talking to this woman named Anice, and in the context of something, I forget what, she mentioned the late visionary, scholar and author Terence McKenna. I said, "You knew Terence McKenna?" She said yes, she was his neighbor in CA, and she collaborated on a project with him also.

I said–my dear, let's go over to the couch and have a nice long chat! And we did.

Speaking of obscure figures in esoteric philosophy– Joel brings this Swedish chick to the party. She's talking with Gil and somehow the name Maurice Nicoll pops up. She is amazed, because she has never, ever, met anyone else who has even HEARD of Maurice Nicoll (including Joel), much less read his books. And we were like, girlfriend, EVERYONE here knows Maurice Nicoll.

So there you have it, another harbinger of the Aquarian Age– where synchronicities abound, and we all read each others' minds, all the time!

HACKING THE DICTIONARY

Deb, thanks for your guestbook post: those voices are scary. Ahhhhh, the fine line between comedy and tragedy. And your word 'cripe' reminds me of another word my Auntie used to say: "criminy" (accent on first syllable).

My brother says that all dictionaries put made-up words in, so they can tell if another dictionary company steals their stuff. Criminy!

JUST WHEN YOU THOUGHT

Just when you thought
someone was watching
it became dark

Just when you thought
someone was listening
you realized
you were alone

Just when you thought
the sun had set
in the east
Just when you thought
the clouds were mountains
Just when you thought
you were floating
on a great ship
instead of driving
on this lousy highway
Just when you thought
a bird flew down
to say hello
Just when you thought
someone called your name
Just when you thought
someone knocked on the door
Just when you thought
you opened the door
and someone came in
and it was the person
you'd been waiting for

Terry

Just when you thought
the question was about
to be answered
and the song was ready
to be sung
and the ocean was coming
to swallow the shore
Just when you tried
to dot an "o"
and cross an "l"
and the letter "g" wriggled
its way out of the pen
like a wild beast
run amok
Just when the smell of meat
crept under the door
and the trees outside
became utterly still

Suddenly there was
no object to be seen
no sound to be heard
no word to be spoken

And a fragile understanding
took hold of your heart
only to vanish
with the very next beat
so that it was not even
a memory
or a feeling
or a notion

Just a flutter of a moth's wings
on the very last ray of moonlight
before dawn

BACK TO SERIOUS STUFF

I call this era we are living in "No More White Picket Fence." It's my reference to the idea espoused by a percussionist colleague whose whole thing was getting the wife, 2.5 kids, and the house with the white picket fence around the yard.

Which reminds me. . . Years ago someone mentioned in conversation that a mutual friend of ours was seeing a shrink for his emotional issues, and the shrink had told him to keep saying to himself: "the world is a safe place. . . the world is a safe place. . . "

That's why I never went to a shrink.

Lest we forget, on September 11, 2001 there was absolutely gorgeous weather.

I just give you the information. You have to decide what to do with it.

GRANDMA & GRANDPA

We were searching for colored glass bottles in Pennsylvania. Gil is insisting that we keep olive oil, water and other liquids and leftovers in glass rather than plastic, and you can find a lot of unusual bottles in antique stores– especially the junkier ones, not the high-end ones. A lot of these old glass jars and bottles have measurement markings on them, in addition to the cool retro logos and such that are so in vogue nowadays.

But the best part was the proprietor, who regaled us with stories about her childhood. Somehow we got to talking about cod liver oil. She said her mother always made her have it every morning, so she didn't care that it's made with a nice lemon flavoring now, she's having none of it.

Her Grandpa had a different tonic for maintaining the kids' health: beer and Alka-Seltzer.

Grandma's cooking was evidently preferred as well. The proprietor remarked: "When mama was cooking, we had oatmeal for breakfast. When Grandma was in charge, we had cookies."

HALLOWEEN & COSTUMES

The whole Halloween thing is a trip. I remember, as a kid, enjoying the excuse to collect and eat candy. My brother, on the other hand, used to hoard his stash–so by the time the next Halloween came around, he still had the candy from the previous year.

Of course, I understand the shelf life of these items rivals that of plutonium.

We're adults here (kids–this site is rated R–do your parents/caretakers/guardians/nannies/legislators/child protection agencies know you're here?) so we don't need to draw unceasing parallels to life on this topic. Suffice it to say that when my mother gave me her china set when I was forty, hell, I had my peanut butter and jelly sandwich on it the very next day! The point being that it's far more fun to be an adult on Halloween, because you can wear a costume and people will indulge you. You can also have fun pretending that other costumed entities really are what they are dressed as.

This past Halloween night, I was having dinner with a bunch of friends at Raoul's, in the heart of Greenwich Village. The Village is home to the world famous Halloween

Inside the Mind of a Musician

Parade. The street and the restaurant were jumping all night. I really enjoyed King Kong (less than life-size stature notwithstanding) picking up various female passersby and running around the sidewalk with them over his shoulder. Their screams were very lifelike!

My dinner was not a costume event, but rest assured, I do have a great costume waiting in the wings. In keeping with my life's role as Creative Improviser and outside-the-box Thinker (who, incidentally, does not sit ergonomically-challenged and naked *à la* Rodin, but rather stands properly aligned and robed *à la* Cheng Man-Ching), my costume has a base outfit which evolves over the course of the evening. Ergo, the outfit is the same, but different, every time. Sort of like playing a tune. But that's enough hints. If you want to see my costume, you will just have to invite me to a costume party.

Years ago I attended a lecture at the Open Center by author and New York University professor James Carse. He had written a fascinating book called Finite and Infinite Games that I absolutely devoured, so I had to go hear him speak.

During the lecture he told a great story about being asked by his students to play the part of a policeman in a school production. Wearing his outfit on the way to dress rehearsal, he was prevailed upon to give directions to several wandering tourists and help an old lady across the street, among other things.

Upon finishing the rehearsal and walking back to his apartment, he remarked how relieved he was to be able to take off the policeman's uniform. He did not like being a policeman. To celebrate his freedom from being a policeman, he put on his regular clothes (jeans, Oxford button-down shirt, tweed jacket, loafers) and went back

Terry

outside. In his quest to affirm his "real" identity once again, he realized that he had merely exchanged the costume of a policeman for the costume of a professor!

RIFFING ON A SUNDAY AFTERNOON HAIKU

Sunday afternoon
Dog drinks from his water bowl
It's going to rain

Sunday afternoon
Grass needs to be mowed today
Do it tomorrow

Sunday afternoon
Someone's smoking a cigar
Should I shoot him now

They say smoking's bad for your health
You could get shot
It's Sunday and in the morning
It'll be Monday
Which stinks because even if
I don't have anything to do
For everyone else it's a workday
And the energy is this
Nine-to-five bustle
And it completely ruins the vibe
You dig?

Sunday afternoon
Used to be when Dad was home

Inside the Mind of a Musician

And he'd be stretched out
On the couch with his headphones on
Listening to some weird music
Or else WQXR
And he'd be reading the Sunday Times

Those were happy times but
"No more white picket fence"
Is what I say nowadays

The world was always a dangerous place
But if you had a white picket fence
You were protected

These days a white picket fence
Is just not enough

So we pretend and play
With our illusions
Like children with blocks
And toy trucks
We have to do that
It's the only way to get through
And come out the other side

The other side of
The white picket fence on a
Sunday afternoon

Terry

HAIR SALON 101

I stopped going to my old hair salon in Greenwich Village because it was run by two moms with little kids and all they had there to read was, like, Parent Magazine.

Nothing against, kids, parents, etc. But when one is at the hair salon, part of that experience is entering oneself, if only temporarily, in the Great Dog Show of Life. When one leaves the hair salon, one will parade one's plumage down the street like a veritable French Poodle, all gussied up with a brand-new melon-scented coiffure.

So to get into the spirit of the thing, you really need to prep by gazing at anorexic models, both hairbrushed and airbrushed. This is New York, after all.

The late Ramesh Durbal used to say that a person's hair is their ego.

Ergo: one's self esteem is in direct proportion to the state of one's hair.

So when I'm getting set to gait through the West Village, that Westminster of human dog shows, the last thing I want to read is Parent Magazine. No. I want to read– Vogue! Harper's, Elle! Hell–I'll even settle for Architectural Digest. But not Parent Magazine. In a hair salon in the Village, not even parents want to read that.

MARCH TOWARD MATRIARCHY? START WITH THE LADIES ROOM

"We are perhaps on the first step to a matriarchal society; women will earn more money than men if current trends continue by 2028," says Michael J. Silverstein of the Boston Consulting Group.

Inside the Mind of a Musician

This quote is from an article in last Sunday's Times. It seems that a home builder in Canada had a sudden epiphany and decided to ask a bunch of women how his kitchens should be designed.

Of course, the women told him his kitchens stunk and they redesigned them for him–probably for free.

Well, I think it's very interesting that this Mr. Silverstein gauges our march toward matriarchy in terms of money–a typically male point of reference.

If I may hypothesize for a moment: in my humble female opinion, the reason women are in control of spending decisions is simply that it's a way to have power without banging your head against the wall trying to get ahead in the boy clubs.

For instance, there are a lot of women entering politics on the township and city level, but as you approach the national level, their numbers decrease dramatically. Same in business (although that seems to be changing at a faster rate.) And definitely the same in the music business.

Women have been slow to enter the traditionally male fields because, at the end of the day, we've cleaned the house, cooked, done the laundry, taken care of the kids, walked the dog, gone to work or school, counseled a suicidal friend, volunteered at the homeless shelter and overhauled the transmission on the Caterpillar, and we're just too tired to run for Congress.

Anyway, now that we've got the kitchen issue taken care of, could we move on to hotel ladies' rooms?

I guess having the counters so big you can't see in the mirror to fix your makeup is to increase business for the staff chiropractor. But the unflattering lighting really stumps me. If I like how I look in the ladies room mirror, then I will feel good about myself. If I feel good about myself, I will spend more money in the place. If I spend more money, the owners will get richer. If the owners are men, we're done. If the owners are women. . . then maybe we wouldn't have the problem in the first place.

Marching towards matriarchy? I'll believe it when I see more stalls at New York's Town Hall. And a Venus of Willendorf in every lobby.

THE SICKENING QUOTIDITY OF REALITY

The sickening quotidity of reality.

But it's not REAL reality.
It's not the reality I signed up for.

To deal with the über-reality
of the worldly world
I have to filter out
more and more each day.

The miracle of my calico cat's fur,
for example.
Each little hair shining with a
luminosity equal to the
stars themselves—
equaling them in number too,
most likely

But the five minutes I used up
petting this luscious creature
could have been put to better,
busier use.

Inside the Mind of a Musician

Possibly by some bureaucrat
at the DMV.

You mean I have to wait in line
just to turn in my plates?

Who's your boss?
Off with his head!
Oh, it's a lady?
No matter—
long hair looks better
waving at the top of the stake.

Play your flute, Pan,
because Chaos reigns
and you can do nothing
except reflect his glory.

I haven't refused your offer.
You just haven't met my price.

The rage I feel
I turn on myself.
But why should I suffer?
Because hey—you either put yourself
in jail,
or they do it for you.

Remember the day we tossed
the ball around in the park?
One of us got a little mad,
threw a little harder—
but the ball was filled with foam,

some of which peeked out of the
ripped seam,
matching that bit at the corner
of your mouth.

In time my mind may forget today,
but the body remembers.

It must be so—
for if we did not carry
the days with us,
each one etched upon
capillaries and tendons,
never to be erased—
then we would be so light
we would never age.

And then how would
the new souls be born?

SURGEON GENERAL SPEAKS

One of my trusted advisors said I should read today's NY Times article about the Surgeon General of the U.S. It is very interesting. I especially like the part about the Bush administration telling the Surgeon General that he was supposed to mention President Bush at least three times on every page of his speeches.

It reminds me of something I read about Stalin, maybe by Solzhenitsyn or Milovan Djilas, saying that Stalin's speeches regularly received standing ovations that went on for quite a long time because no one wanted to be the first to sit down.

Inside the Mind of a Musician

WHEN HARRY MET ZSA ZSA...

Harry has started his autobiography. An excerpt:

"We're opposites in so many ways: I like the sun, she likes shade. I like wet food, she likes dry. I like to eat late–but she gets too hungry for dinner at eight.

We met in a bathroom during the Westminster show. I was crazy about her right away. Not just 'cause of her looks–her markings, the fringe on her ears, her gorgeous smile. The thing that really got me, I could tell that she was, you know, sincere. And innocent. Not much in the brains department, but hey, I'm no Einstein myself.

Anyway, she went home with me that night. But first we went to a jam session. There were lots of cats there. Not THOSE kind of cats. But she hadn't ever seen either kind. Boy, was she in for a surprise..."

PAULO COELHO

I was surfing in iTunes and discovered that Paulo Coelho's book The Alchemist can be downloaded in audiobook form (read by Jeremy Irons) for 95 cents.

I know a deal when I see one.

The Alchemist is a charming story; it captured me right away, from the prologue on. Coelho calls it a fable, and it is written in a simple style, but full of wisdom.

Kind of like, Hemingway meets Thich Nhat Hahn.

Last night, inspired by The Alchemist, I jotted down my own humble homage to Coelho's fable. Here it is:

When I was young I wrote a short story about a girl with an elephant head. She got the elephant head from reading too much. She wanted to remember everything she

Terry

had ever read, and this storing of information in her brain made her brain–and thus her skull itself–expand into a gargantuan size.

One reads something–a little snippet of wisdom–or a phrase of delicate beauty–and one feels illumined. One wishes to always remember the words and have them at one's command when one would like to have that feeling again.

For it is not the phrase, or the idea, but rather the feeling one gets from contemplating the idea, that is stimulating.

But there are many such phrases, and one either hasn't a pen, or doesn't have time to stop and jot it down. But in any case, one is certain to remember the words; how could one forget?

And thus the words are forgotten in an hour's time, or a day. It doesn't matter. Even if one wanted to remember everything, it would be impossible.

It is better, then, to live as if the words will come at the right time, when they are most needed. Instead of trying to remember all the beautiful and wise words I've ever heard, I will trust that they will appear just at the right moment. And that is when they will truly belong to me. I will use them and get that feeling, and go on with my day.

Herein lies the power of a song–and the danger.

A song makes the words keep going; they can ride forever on the melody, like a wave that keeps running up on the shore. It's not the same wave, of course–or is it? Is not that wave a part of the ocean–making all waves the same? They're all pieces of the same ocean, playing the same song, over and over again.

A HALF CENTURY OF MAGAZINE SUBSCRIPTIONS

As a youngster in the idealistic and turbulent 60's, I subscribed to the Weekly Reader. My mom paid.

Growing up in the Watergate 70's, I subscribed to Mad Magazine. My mom paid.

Coming of age in the 80's, an era that wanted to be the 60's but was too square, I subscribed to the Utne Reader with my own hard-earned cash.

Rebutting the excesses of the 80's were the postmodern and health-clubbed 90's, during which I subscribed to Wired.

And here we are in the 00's, seemingly quite far away from the Age of Aquarius, so I subscribe to American Rifleman.

SUNDAY TIMES TIDBITS

Some interesting articles in the Sunday Times "Week in Review" section. John Markoff writes about the New Internet: "The Internet's original designers never foresaw that the academic and military research network they created would one day bear the burden of carrying all the world's communications and commerce . . . little attention was given to security."

Markoff suggests that a re-designed Internet would require its users to prove their identity, rather than surf anonymously as we do now. So, just as one needs a passport to cross international borders, similar indemnity will be required to travel through cyber space. And if you are a web addict, as many of us now are, then you will go for it. But let us note that as long as individuals have control over anything, there will always be crime. Crime cannot be erased until every individual freedom is revoked. And who will be doing the revoking, I wonder. Surely that task will fall to our Big Brother, 'cause he's so good at it.

Lest anyone wonder where all these security measures are heading–in the inexorable march toward a compulsory national (and eventually global) identity chip implementation program, that's where I get off the bus.

Don't be dismayed. Even Pandora's Box carried a tiny creature called Hope. In Thomas L. Friedman's article on the Opinion page he describes a recent tour of India undertaken by two young ladies in a partial-electric car with a solar roof. Driving down Panchsheel Marg, they point out the roof of the U.S. Embassy (covered with surveillance equipment), and that of the Chinese Embassy, covered with solar hot water heaters. Their tour became a consciousness-raising "climate caravan" complete with dancers, art, and a band with solar-powered amplifiers.

If the U.S. keeps tanking, I think I'll open a chain of American restaurants in China. Americans won't be able to afford to live here anymore, and there will be mass emigration. So there won't be any shortage of Americans to work in my restaurants, cheap. As far as benefits, they don't have health care here, so they certainly won't expect it there– another savings for management!

Following the current model of user-generated content ("screw the Writers Guild, we'll program more reality shows!") I'm now accepting menu suggestions. Forward your resume to me while you're at it–I'm looking for a Head Dishwasher.

A NEW POEM

There once was a girl named Su
Whose bizarre ruminations were due
To her keen sense of humor
Or else a brain tumor
Or perhaps just an ill-fitting shoe.

REFLECTIONS ON TRAVIS

Travis was a chimpanzee who basically lived life like a human being: feeding, bathing and dressing himself, surfing cable channels and quaffing down a glass of wine with his steak dinner. He lived with a widow named Sandra Herold, who said the chimp "couldn't have been more my son than if I gave birth to him." (in the New York Times piece, check out the hilarious illustration by Peter Arkle–note the bottle of Nair behind the Neanderthal's chair!)

One day, Travis became highly agitated for no apparent reason. Mrs. Herold made him a cup of tea laced with Xanax to calm him down, but it only made him worse. When a friend came over to help, Travis severely mauled him. The police came and shot Travis dead.

The pundits started saying: Chimps are wild animals. They are dangerous and shouldn't live with humans.

Like humans don't ever go berserk?

It's now thought that Travis might have had an illness, and that the Xanax induced a psychotic state (as it can do to humans as well.)

Goodness knows there are all manner of emotionally-based or illness-based reasons for aggression and even temporary insanity, in any animal species including homo sapiens. Why, not long ago, my car mechanic was practically taken away in a straight jacket when a virus he had contracted made its way into his brain.

He's fine now. Still overcharging.

In a perfect world, maybe Travis could have gotten the benefit of the doubt. But if this world is about anything, it's The Luck of the Draw.

Sorry, Travis—you drew the Chimp Card.

WILD TURKEY COURTSHIP RITUAL

Please be advised that the following is neither a liquor advertisement nor an instruction manual. It is just what the title says: a description of what I believe to be a typical courtship ritual performed by wild turkeys in the woods near my Pennsylvania studio.

Driving by a small clearing in the woods by the side of the road, I observed four male turkeys in full regalia. If you have never seen this, it is a sight to behold. You may, when seeing this for the first time, mistake the turkeys for peacocks. The males have beautiful colors on their heads and necks, that combine with their fanned-out tail feathers in a magnificent display.

The females are rather dull-looking in comparison, but they do have one thing that the males want.

Normally, turkeys will not hang around when people or cars approach. They don't exactly run away, but they do waddle rather quickly and intently in the opposite direction. On this occasion, the male turkeys stood their ground, obviously engaged in the very important contest of vying for the one female's attention.

Not only did they stand their ground when the car drove by, backed up, and sat there with a human watching from inside—but they did it defiantly, tail feathers spread, as if to demonstrate to Miss Turkey that they possess that all-important quality of Courage.

If I am not mistaken, it is definitely in the best interests of wild turkeys to flee from humans, being that humans have been their predators at least since the Pilgrims landed on these shores some four centuries ago.

Therefore, I deduce that the male turkeys were so involved in their courtship ritual of the only female present that they completely ignored the proximity of a possible natural predator—namely, me.

I am led to the conclusion that, even in the wild, males still do really stupid things to impress females.

On the other hand–the female wasn't going anyplace either . . .

CREDO

Sometimes one needs an idea, or a story, to keep going amongst the 'slings and arrows of outrageous fortune.' It's been said: sometimes you need a story more than you need food.

Why should we not live our lives as if they were of mythic proportions? The stuff of myth is all around us, be it exalted or ever so humble.

ENGLISH

I've always had this strange ability to know how a word is spelled. I can spot a spelling error a mile away–they just jump out at me. I don't consider it a talent–it's more like an idiot savant kind of thing.

It would have perhaps been more auspicious to have had a talent for picking lottery numbers, or stocks, or

Terry

racehorses. But I don't mean to sound ungrateful. At least I know if the music thing doesn't work out, I could always fall back on a $15/hour proofreading job.

The irony is, in your nocturnal, dream life, you're screwed no matter what. As a proofreader, my dreams would be about bungling an important document and losing millions of dollars for the company; whereas now, all I need to do is find the missing pieces of my clarinet. Sometimes, they even turn up.

OK, POETRY LOVERS...

(I made this one with the "poetry kit fridge magnets"):

She worships a shadow,
he is the wind and rain;
rocks her like some sad ship
in an enormous storm
then crushes her like a sweet peach
in a lather of drool and sweat

Beneath this fluff of sky
a languid symphony of whispers
rose to a boil
and a still sleep licked away
love milk from your hair
with shadows from the cooling sun

21ST CENTURY AMERICAN KOAN

All I want to do is live my life–but my life keeps getting in the way.

Inside the Mind of a Musician

TECH DIFFICULTIES, PLEASE STAND BY

Terry

TECH DIFFICULTIES, PLEASE STAND BY

I was using Avery AfterBurner software to make CD labels, but they weren't selling it anymore at the place I go (which I refuse to name because why should I give them free advertising, although I could add some negative comments which would perhaps erase the effect of the free advertising, and perhaps even give me a refreshing sense of revenge EVEN THOUGH THEY SAY LIVING WELL IS THE BEST REVENGE but anyway there's enough negativity in the world already don't you think) so I had to buy Memorex. After I got over my frustration at having to figure out a new template, which took a couple of hours, I actually like the Memorex better. Which is why they've gotten two product placements in this paragraph. But don't necessarily rush out and buy it, because it's not perfect, believe me.

SOLSTICE

OK, it's the summer solstice–so, did anyone else try to do the egg thing?

EQUINOX

The Equinox? Duh! So that's why it didn't work!

A RIDE BY ANY OTHER NAME

My brother Brian said he took the family to a country fair in Pennsylvania. It was advertised "All Rides

Free!" When they got to the fairgrounds, there were a whole bunch of rides. But only five of them were called "rides." The rest were called "attractions." You have to pay for attractions.

Maybe I'm old-fashioned, but that seems kind of slimy.

RETRACTION

Previously in this blog, I reported that spraying oneself with Listerine appeared to be an effective mosquito repellent. I am afraid that after continued field research, however, my assertion appears not to be borne out.

Or, it could be that the Listerine did work at first, but these East Coast mosquitos, accustomed as they are to combating all manner of repellents–commercial and otherwise–have quickly developed a resistance to it.

Moreover, they appear to be biting with even more ferocity than before. I think they like the Listerine–it gets the taste of blood out of their mouth.

BAKING BREAD

No, this is not a cutesy title regarding counterfeiting. This post is actually about–baking bread!

Although some folks may be surprised to know that amongst my friends and family I am fairly renowned for my culinary talents, I must admit that for bread, I do use a bread machine. It's a Zojirushi and it works great.

So I'm in a Poconos supermarket, searching for active dry yeast. Searching, searching. Why is it not in the aisle with the flour? I seek out the manager, who says yeast is located in the dairy section. Even there it's hard to spot, but I find it. Mind you, active dry yeast does not need refrigeration.

I go back and tell the manager that it should be in the aisle with the flour.

He says that every store he ever worked in, it's in the dairy section.

And to this I say: Just because that's the way you've always done it, doesn't mean it's right.

IT AIN'T EASY BEING A FILL IN THE BLANK

The mail carrier has been dumping the mail for the whole building in my mailbox. So I have to stand out there in the cold, sifting through it and putting it in the correct boxes.

Lying in wait for the mail carrier today, I listened for the telltale mailbox squeak followed by a too-quick gate slam that would indicate he had not bothered to put the mail in its proper place.

I went out. Sure enough, my box was practically overflowing, and it's a big box.

I call out to the mailman. He says, "Oh, sorry" and he keeps walking down the street! I'm like, no, excuse me, I'm not going to do your job for you. Could you please come back here and deliver the mail, like you're supposed to?

So he comes back, and he says, "I have to be back by a certain time. You don't know what it's like being a mailman."

I thought of saying, "Yeah, and you don't know what it's like being a paroled homicidal maniac whose meds ran out two weeks ago" but I didn't.

Inside the Mind of a Musician

GENDER MISIDENTIFICATION

Call me ignorant (go ahead, make my day) but I learned something today.

I know that George Sand was a woman, and Evelyn Waugh was a man.

I know that Charles and Ray Eames were not brothers, but husband and wife. (Ray was Mrs. Eames.)

But I did not know that Flannery O'Connor was a woman!

According to Wikipedia, O'Connor's passion was ornithology, though not in the key of G. She once said: "When I was six I had a chicken that walked backward and was in the Pathe News. I was in it too with the chicken. I was just there to assist the chicken but it was the high point in my life. Everything since has been anticlimax."

I kinda felt the same way after teaching myself how to whistle with my hands. It took me hours of practicing on the bus after school. To my ten-year-old self, It felt really good to have accomplished such a difficult, completely unmarketable skill. But now that I'm a grownup...well...I guess nothing much has changed.

WHEN THEY SAY "CONTROL TOP" THEY AIN'T KIDDIN'

Speaking of chick hairdos, don't get me started on the topic of chick clothes.

Ladies, you are familiar with the phenomenon known as "control top", as applied to a wide variety of panty-hose-type items. Guys–get a chick to explain it to you if you're clueless: basically what we're going for here is

Terry

erasure of "lines", whether they be due to undergarments, static electricity, or trajectories of *avoirdupois*. Suffice it to say that the invention of the "control top" has given new hope to those chicks who do not have the benefit of an Art Dept. to airbrush them into the chick clothes so ruthlessly foisted upon them by an anorexic-worshipping fashion industry.

Of course, the Control Top technology has been striving to keep pace with parallel developments in other fields. So what we now have is "Weapons Grade Control Top." Dang, I sprained my wrist this morning trying to get on a pair of CT capris to wear under my Nike running pants for this video shoot. There should be a warning on the box: "This Product May Be Dangerous To Your Soft Tissue. Consult Your Doctor Prior To Use."

Or afterwards.

FISH STORY

So this afternoon I took myself to the beach, way out on Long Island, past Jones Beach to one called Cedar Beach. It's off season so you don't have to pay $20 to park. It was a great beach day, and there was hardly anyone there. Around sunset this fisherman comes over to me with a big fish and offers it to me, he said he caught too many and couldn't carry it. It was a 10 lb. striped bass. They go for $12/lb in the store. I was like, I don't know what to do with this. He says, "Take it to Shop Rite, they'll clean it for you." He thought I was a local.

I couldn't see leaving this beautiful fish on the beach, so I wrapped it in a towel and took it with me. I didn't know where Shop Rite was, but I figured, how hard can it be to clean a fish? I'll look it up on the Internet!

While I'm driving on the Meadowbrook Parkway, I'm thinking, gee, it would be nice to share this fish with someone, and Gil wasn't home, so I checked my messages to see if any of my friends called while I was out. Yes! Elysa called to give me a gig! "Hello, Elysa–what are you doing right now?"

"Cutting vegetables."

"Great, I've got the main course, I'll be right over."

Then there was the problem of how to clean the fish, which neither one of us knew anything about. The fish stores were closed. I called my friend who's a surgeon at Mt. Sinai, but she wasn't available. The local Rabbi (he's great at a bris) couldn't make it either. Then Elysa's husband Wayne showed up, who in addition to his many other talents (and to the surprise of his wife) was an expert fish cleaner.

Yeah, it was good. And now I know how to clean a fish. You have to have a sharp knife.

HEY–DON'T TOUCH THE ANTENNAE

I just have to say, for the record, that I think these Bluetooth headsets that people wear on their ears in public are the zenith of Dorkdom.

Yes, I realize the convenience of having a one-piece unit that clips onto your ear so you can talk handsfree on your cellphone. But they seem to have become fashion accessories for the VIP-in-my-own-mind set.

Call me a Luddite (go ahead, I dare you–and we'll duke it out in the back, your PDA against my Post-It Pad) but I don't see any difference between sporting a bluetooth headset and, say, a beanie with a propeller on top.

Terry

In any case, it's out of our hands (pun intended). If the future unfolds as current events would indicate, I'm sure that humans will evolve to accommodate our future survival. In fact, I understand that a baby has already been born in Tokyo with a Bluetooth device seamlessly integrated into the cartilage of the ear.

Mother Nature does know best!

MY LIFE IS GREAT, HOW 'BOUT YOURS?

Holiday parties with bands are largely a thing of the past, I'm afraid.

Except, evidently, for my colleague E, who writes to her e mail list that she feels blessed for her incredible good fortune at being so unbelievable busy with holiday parties, recording sessions, and what have you.

My friend D read this e mail, and decided to write a PARODY of E's e mail, complete with matching fonts and colors. I laughed hysterically when I saw it at a party at her house. Thinking she had written it for her own amusement, I asked if I could have a copy. "Check your e mail," D said. "I sent this to her entire cc list!"

I stopped accepting New Years Eve gigs a while ago, unless I get a really good offer! There are so many drunk people on the road, it's scary. A few years ago I was a half block from my Brooklyn apartment at around 3 a.m., when a car came whizzing through, against the light, right in front of me.

The last NYE gig I did was when I was Musical Director for Roxane Butterfly's tap dance troupe. We had a gig at a church function in Monticello, which is a haul, by the way. So I decided to park my car in Manhattan and ride in the church van with the dance company and the choir members.

We finally get to the gig, and there's no booze. It's a church, right? The food consisted of potato chips and pretzels. The rec room of the church reminded me of the old days of playing polka gigs in VFW halls, only the food was better back then.

After the gig, the van driver drove us back to New York, where he proceeded to drop off every single choir member in front of their respective buildings in Harlem. My car was parked in midtown.

I got home at daybreak. The gig paid well, but not well enough.

And while we're on the subject, I never quite saw the attraction of standing around Times Square with thousands of other freezing people waiting for the ball to come down, while the police infiltrate the crowd looking for terrorists and the guy next to you spills his flask of peppermint schnapps on your jacket.

But that's just me.

SECRET CODE

I finally figured out what the deal is with these spam e mail subject headings–

"delegacy retrospective"

"Re: decanter dessert"

"A fix the considering sprout"

"ingered for an hour"

People–beware! What can this be other than terrorist secret codes!

I will probably be arrested just for reprinting them here. But that's okay, I need the publicity.

Terry

COMPUTER CAPER GONE WRONG

I know it's Christmas. I know. You probably think I don't have a life, blogging on Christmas Day and all.

Well nyah nyah, it just so happens that I'm going to a party in forty-five minutes! Just thought I'd sit down for a moment and share with you a bonehead blunder I committed last night, for your amusement and possible edification.

We bought two new MacBooks. But Gil has a program that he likes that only works in Windows. So I thought I'd hook up Apple's utility called Boot Camp that allows you to run Windows on a Mac.

The instructions clearly said, you must have a Windows installation disk, not a download, containing Service Pack 2.

Well, who has a disc with Service Pack 2? No one. Because Service Pack 2 was a download from Microsoft–it didn't come on the first editions of XP. Those discs had Service Pack 1.

When I'm cooking, if I don't have a certain spice or something that's called for in the recipe, I just substitute something else. No thyme? Use mint! No milk? Use half 'n half! Whatever. It's improvisation, man!

So I'm like, Service Pack 1, Service Pack 2, same difference.

I install Windows in the Mac. It installs fine until I get the Blue Screen of Death that hangs there until I have to hold the power button to shut it down. When I power on again in Windows, it wouldn't recognize the Mac OS disc with the Boot Camp utility on it.

So now the Mac will only boot up in Windows. If I were in the city I could go to the Apple Store that's open 24/7 (yes even on Christmas) but I'm not, so if I can't resolve this over the phone tomorrow, I guess I will have to bring it in.

In the midst of this fiasco, I decided, belatedly, to Google this situation, thereby learning that such a feat had been attempted by others who met a similar fate.

There was one site that said you could "slipstream" Service Pack 2 into a new disc. The instructions were from here to the traffic light in Canadensis.

Whenever I contemplate undertaking a task like this, I always invoke Einstein's famous equation, $T=M$.

Time equals Money.

Good thing I bought the extended warranty with the Bonehead Computer-Dilettante provision.

CECIL PAYNE

Cecil Payne, the great baritone saxophonist, died on Tuesday. Tim Price just sent me an e mail reminiscing about some good times playing with Cecil over the years.

One time, in the eighties I think, I was sitting in with Cecil at some little dive club in New York. We were playing a tune; everyone had soloed already–the horn players, piano, bass, drums–and it was time to take the tune out.

I looked over at Cecil, but he was deep in conversation with someone. So I played the melody and we took the tune out.

Cecil was livid! He said, how dare you come on my bandstand and take the tune out! I take the tune out, not you!

I was completely flummoxed. I was a young player with a lot more experience with music than with politics. I didn't understand the finer points of bandstand diplomacy! All I knew was that it was time for someone to play the melody, and he was busy, so I played it.

Well, I was crushed that Cecil had yelled at me. I must have slunked (slinked? slanked?) away with my tail between my legs, because he later came over and apologized profusely, saying he had had a bad day and got a little overwrought.

But I realized that he was right–it wasn't my place to take the tune out. It wasn't my gig. So I learned an important lesson. Yeah, it's about the music–but music is a team sport and it's also about respecting everyone's role on the bandstand.

DRESSING ROOMS, OR LACK THEREOF

Did you know that many of the New York jazz clubs lack decent dressing rooms for their artists?
("NO! I hear you gasp).

It's true.

The venerable Village Vanguard, for instance, has no dressing room. The artists hang out in an old kitchen, seated on folding chairs (if you can find one) surrounded by decrepit stoves, sinks and countertops. I suppose it qualifies as a sort of "green room", although it is not private. Pretty much anyone can walk in there.

Sweet Rhythm has no room for the artists at all. Zilch, not even a kitchen. And unless you're a Yoga teacher, heaven help you if you've got to change in that bathroom. Better you should sprint across the street to the Mexican place. If it's not raining.

Inside the Mind of a Musician

The dressing room at Dizzy's Club is the size of a walk-in closet. But at least there is comfortable seating and a bathroom.

The Minton's green room is an office. A very small office, with a whole lot of stuff in there. Be sure to hermetically seal your belongings before using it.

Birdland is okay if you don't have to go from one end of the dressing room to the other– to the bathroom, for instance. The room is shaped like a hallway, so if other band members are in there, traversing it is like navigating aisles in a movie theater. But a movie theater aisle is easier because you don't have to leap over horn cases.

The Blue Note has real dressing rooms that are small, but private and clean. They don't double as storage rooms. There is one for the bandleader, and another for the band. And at those prices, I would expect no less.

These are just a few clubs that come to mind.

(Is the Complaint Dept. open yet? I've been on 'hold' such a long time) PLEASE SUMMARIZE YOUR COMPLAINT IN 60 WORDS OR LESS

Not having a dressing room/green room is a drag because:

1. Must change and put on makeup in public bathroom (so much for that 'artist mystique' you were trying to cultivate... now EVERYONE knows you use Maybelline Instant Age Rewind)

2. No place to sit down and look over music or warm up (hey, you knew about this gig two weeks ago!)

3. No place to be away from the public to chill out between sets (are you some kind of prima donna, or what)

Terry

4. Where are you supposed to count the money and pay the musicians after the job (just go in the bathroom to count the money, drug dealers don't seem to have a problem with that so why should you)

THANK YOU, YOUR COMPLAINT WILL BE PROCESSED IN FOUR TO EIGHT WEEKS.

I like interacting with my fans and friends who come to the show, but I need a clean and quiet place to go for all of the above. I put out lots of energy when I play, and I can do a better job when I don't have to spend more energy talking to people between sets. This is very draining. I prefer to save my energy for performing, and chat with folks AFTER the gig.

Let's not forget that most of these clubs would have zero customers if not for the artists performing there. Few seem to realize this, least of whom the artists themselves.

Now that I think about it, if all clubs provided clean, private dressing rooms for their artists, the artists might start to think more of themselves, and get all uppity, and demand more money!

Oh. . . I get it now.

REPLACE CAPACITOR ON CIRCUIT BOARD, PIECE OF CAKE

Gil's hobby is recording commercial-free films from the Turner Classic Movies channel, so the demise of the Panasonic DVD recorder came as a blow. No power, no "hello", nothing. It was a death so sudden that he feared he'd never see the DVD that was inside it again.

Inside the Mind of a Musician

Apparently the death of the recorder was due to a common problem: a faulty capacitor. Easy enough to fix, said a guy on the Internet, and he gave oral instructions and pictures on how to proceed.

Gil said, "We can do this." I gave my standard reply: "What you mean "we", white man?" (That's the punchline to joke #138 featuring the Lone Ranger and Tonto.)

Gil assembled the required materials: Phillips screwdriver, soldering pen, roll of solder, small brush for clearing away bits of old solder. First step–take off five screws and slide the Panasonic's cover back.

The people over at Panasonic made it be known that they would really prefer you did not remove their cover by cementing in the two final screws.

After I got the !@#$%$#@^**&% cover off, it was smooth sailing. I just needed to ID the faulty capacitor, then I proceeded to unscrew the circuit board and de-solder the underside of the capacitor leads to remove it.

My spiritual practices really came in handy here, as you need the patience of Job to wait till the soldering pen reaches the solder-melting point, which it evidently does in random, unpredictable bursts. Did you know that as soon as solder melts, it hardens again? It was a bit like when Dorothy threw water on the Wicked Witch of the West; she melted, but she left a pile of clothes and a pointy witch's hat on the floor.

I finally removed enough solder to jiggle the capacitor loose with a pair of pliers. I inserted the new capacitor, taking pains to orient the negative lead to face the black doohickey thing.

Oh, I forgot to mention that I had to separate this other wired thingamabob before I could take the circuit board off in the first place–that was no picnic either.

Next step: soldering the leads of the new capacitor to the underside of the circuit board. This part was very similar to operating a caulking gun, that is, if you are Gulliver in the Land of the Lilliputians.

Finally everything was in place and the device was ready to be turned on. Imagine our disappointment when we pressed the power button and nothing happened. Imagine our glee when we realized it was unplugged.

"Is there a reward attached to this caper?" I asked Gil.

"What do you have in mind?" he replied.

"How about a Piaggio BV250 motor scooter?"

"I have a better idea" he said, and my heart skipped a beat.

Dinner and a movie it is.

GIGABYTES?

I think a gigabyte is bigger than a megabyte but I'm not sure. To tell you the truth, I'm still working on how many quarts to a gallon.

TRANSPOSING: TRY IT AT HOME FIRST

I just received an e mail from a new alto saxophone convert named Richard. He writes that he is trying to learn how to read music, and is using my book Step One: Play Alto Sax to get started on the horn.

I have an exercise near the beginning of the book, in which the student holds out some tones, tuning the notes to me playing on the accompanying CD.

Inside the Mind of a Musician

Richard held up an electronic tuner to the speaker, and was surprised to find that the note names it displayed were not the same ones he was playing. But he was in tune with the CD, so what gives?

In their zeal to play the instrument, there are probably many students who skip over boring text like that on page 10, where mention is made of the fact that the alto saxophone's note names are not in "concert pitch." Concert pitch refers to the pitches of instruments in the key of C–like piano, oboe, flute, and most string family instruments.

This is actually a sinister plot that was concocted in centuries past, to keep people out of the music business. It doesn't seem to have worked.

But it HAS served to fry the brains of many a neophyte arranger and composer. Though nowadays, you can just push the "transpose" button on your computer–and voila, you don't have to learn to write the viola part in viola clef.

Actually, are there even C clefs on notation programs? There must be. But since I am a hopeless luddite, scrawling my way across the manuscript paper with an actual pencil, I have no idea.

Anyway, I thought that some of you might be interested in this arcane bit of musicology, so here's what I wrote to Richard:

The alto saxophone is pitched in Eb, not C. Most tuners only display what is known as "concert pitch", referring to instruments pitched in C, like the piano.

We say an alto sax is pitched in Eb because when it plays its C, it's an Eb on the piano. Likewise, a tenor sax, trumpet or clarinet is pitched in Bb because when they play their C, it's a Bb on the piano.

Terry

Let's say we want the alto to play the note C, along with the piano. If the alto plays its C, it will really be an Eb. So if you want the alto to be playing the same note as the piano, you have to raise the alto's note C by a Major 6th. (the difference between Eb and C.) Then you will be playing your note A, sounding at the same pitch as the piano's C.

If this sounds confusing, it's because it is. Even pros get mixed up sometimes, and transpose in the wrong direction!

Of course, this situation begs the question: How did all this come to pass?

The origin of all this transposition business comes from the fact that when the wind instruments were invented, they were designed to play only in certain keys. Before and even during the lifetime of J.S. Bach, who was a big proponent of "equal tempered" tuning (meaning that all the half steps in a chromatic scale are basically the same distance apart), there were other tuning systems that were in competition to become the standard system.

The adoption of equal temperament as the standard tuning system in Western Europe–and thus the U.S.–enabled all the instruments to be able to play with each other in any key.

Even so, we must keep in mind that only a keyboard or mallet percussion instrument can be a truly tempered instrument. String and wind instruments, when they are not playing along with a piano, will display a much more varied range of temperament.

Some musicians are of the opinion that a long period of piano music is more fatiguing to the ear than music performed on winds, strings, or voice. While the equal temperament system has many advantages, it does in fact alter the relationships of the tones as they naturally occur in the overtone series.

If you've read this far, you show potential for the Music Geek of the Year award, a little-known subdivision of the Nobel Prize. Advance two squares, and read "Temperament" by Stuart Isacoff.

HERE I GO AGAIN

I'm going to try and make this short, because I can't stand conspiracy theories that ramble on and on–what about you?

There are a number of companies doing genetic testing: DeCODEme and Navigenics are two of the leaders in the field, and now the startup 23andMe is getting a lot of publicity. (23 is the number of pairs of chromosomes in humans.)

The recent New York Times article on the new company–interestingly, relegated to the "Styles" section, along with celebrity sightings and cocktail recipes–briefly noted that 23andMe's co-founder, Anne Wojcicki, is "the wife of a founder of Google."

Hello! So Sergey Brin's wife and, coincidentally, his partner Larry Page's wife, are both in the genetics field! Well, the aristocracy has never held "true love" to be the sole deciding factor in a potential marriage partner, and surely Page and Brin, Kings of the Google Empire, know that queens are always chosen with the expansion of empire in mind. Long live the Kings–with the aid of 23andMe, of course.

I love that DNA analysis has released wrongly-convicted prisoners, and isolated the gene for Huntington's Disease. We also know, however, that anything that has power can be used either for good or for evil. The journey from "genetics" to "eugenics" is, etymologically and otherwise, rather short.

The Google Gang may be all good intentions–I hope so, for all our sakes.

Nevertheless, I sort of think the only reason we're not yet cowering in cubbyholes hiding from our TV sets, like Winston Smith in "1984", is because of the bumbling ineptitude of government.

NOT THE JET PACK OF MY DREAMS

Okay, so Yves Rossy's got a jet pack and he flew over the Alps, the English Channel, and a bunch of other places.

Big deal.

He still had to go up in a plane to start out. What good is that? Listen, Yves: I need a jet pack where, like, I can take off from my driveway! Do you think you could work that one up?

But I guess if you could'a, you would'a.

I'll bet it has something to do with the amount of thrust required to become airborne, if I'm not mistaken. I'll bet you need a whole lotta thrust, which would make the proposition much more dangerous than it is now.

Hey you, put out that cigarette!

The fact of the matter is, if I can't keep the thing in my trunk and use it during traffic jams, then it's practically useless. Because if I want to fly around over fields and whatnot, I can do that while astral traveling, and I don't have to spend for the jet fuel.

YOU & YOUR IPOD

Yes, I am now an iPod convert, after having trashed the iPod both verbally and in print for many years.

And now that I am a devotee, I have acquired a bit of knowledge as to the care and feeding of this inorganic pet.

Recent problem: The "hold" switch was not working. This is a drag because the device needs only a light touch to turn on, so if something touches it while it is stored it may turn on and deplete the battery.

Solution: Reset the iPod. (This will not erase any files or settings.) Do this by powering on the device with the hold switch off, then pressing "Menu" and the middle "select" button simultaneously until you see the Apple logo appear.

The Apple logo will appear as a gigantic luminous holographic haze, taking up most of your field of vision. . .

OOPS no that was a dream I had last night–

Correction, the Apple logo will appear on the screen of the device.

Your iPod is now reset. There is one more thing you need to do: when powering off the device, wait ten seconds before putting the hold switch on.

The hold switch should now work.

The testing device was an iPod 8GB Nano. The old square one, not the new one.

If resetting your device does not solve your problem, you may have to return it to Apple for repair. I understand the turnaround time is short. In the meantime I guess you'll have to amuse yourself by playing with the ringtones on your cell.

Tra la la!

REEDS

As Nelson Hill said to me yesterday:

What's the difference between the Easter Bunny and a good reed?

Answer: The Easter Bunny might actually exist.

SUBWAY COMPLAINTS

I had a gig with Scot at the Lincoln Center Barnes & Noble today. Took the subway. There's a new ad down there, put out by one of the organizations that is protesting fare hikes. The headline is: "At $103 a month, you'd expect they'd have a sauna, a pool and Pilates classes down there."

Well, I hate to ruin a great ad campaign for a worthy cause, but whoever came up with this one obviously hasn't ridden the subway for quite a while.

The fact is, that the MTA does indeed sport saunas on its platforms. They are seasonal, and run from June through August and sometimes into September. Moreover, the price is included in your subway fare!

As far as a pool, why, just head down to the tracks during any downpour–you will find an intricately-designed system of wading pools for your tired, aching feet. The only drawback is that you will have to share them with the rats.

It is true that there are no Pilates classes in the subway, however you will find a wide variety of aerobic activities, including Stairmasters (these are the original, manual style); Yoga and stretching classes (especially during rush hour); and plenty of puzzles and games (particularly when navigating the Times Square station) that will surely keep you occupied.

Now that you mention it, why not cancel that gym membership–it's SO redundant.

Inside the Mind of a Musician

MUSIC RULES

Ronnie writes in about how hard a life it is to be a musician.

Well . . . yeah.

I always encourage kids and young people who are into music, but I would definitely say: do not go into this for a living unless it is your only option.

Being a musician is way cool, particularly being a jazz musician. You get to immerse yourself in the study of a profound and exciting art form. You get paid to travel around the world and meet interesting people.

On a good day, you feel like you're soaring; you're in a trance and the music plays you, not the other way around.

For each one of those rare moments, you will pay dearly. One of the ways you will pay is with all the crap gigs you'll have to do just to get to that one good one that comes along occasionally.

What'll really get you is when you've got a great band and a potentially great set in front of you; only the acoustics are so bad, or the sound person so inept, that you can't hear properly and the gig ends up sucking.

This has happened to me many times.

But you will keep doing it because music rules. Music is awesome, it's fun, it's exciting, it's artistically satisfying. It's like a drug, and it will rule you. It demands much of your life. There are no vacations from music. You will always have music running through your head. You will always have things you need to work on to improve. You will frequently be dissatisfied with your own playing (no matter how good you are.)

Terry

And if you ever stop trying to become an even better musician than you are, you need to get out of the business.

STUDENT AWARD

And this week's Best Student Excuse Award goes to...

the envelope please...

and the winner is...

ED!

I asked him why he was playing a certain rhythm incorrectly, and he said:

"Sorry—one of my synapses isn't firing."

ABOUT THE AUTHOR

Saxophonist, clarinetist and composer Su Terry first heard jazz as a child in Connecticut, where her father had an extensive record collection and she listened to jazz station WRVR FM daily. As a teenager studying with noted pianist and educator John Mehegan, Su contemplated beginning her composing career by writing a big band arrangement for her high school jazz ensemble. Mehegan bet her an ice cream cone she couldn't do it. She won.

Su began her professional music career at the age of 16. Enrolling in the Hartt School of the University of Hartford as a classical clarinetist two years later, her secret agenda was to study saxophone with the late jazz legend Jackie McLean. She graduated with honors and was named the Hartt School Alum of the Year in 2001.

Upon her arrival in New York in the early 1980's, Su became a featured soloist with bands led by jazz masters Charli Persip, Clifford Jordan, Walter Bishop, Jr. and Jaki Byard. She went on to work with greats such as Dr. Billy Taylor, Clark Terry, Peggy Stern, Melba Liston, Hilton Ruiz, Irene Reid, Joe Lee Wilson and Clarice Assad. She's been a jazz soloist with the National Symphony, the Brooklyn Philharmonic, the Hartford Symphony, the New York Pops and the Florida Pops, and performs worldwide. Her discography currently contains over fifty recordings, including four as leader and three as co-leader. She's the author of several music instruction books, three non-fiction books and an illustrated short novel. She is a regular contributor to Allegro Magazine and a columnist for The Note.

In 2014 she wrote and starred in an award-winning documentary short titled "The Source."

Su's other passion is for the martial arts---she is an 8-time USKSF Championship Tournament gold medalist in taijiquan.

Her website is www.suterry.com, where you can download articles, music, see photos and videos and much more.

Su Terry is a Yamaha Saxophone Artist.

"One should almost say that this young lady is born for her instrument. That relaxed, exalted playing! That rhythmic feeling! That improvisational skill! Simply extraordinary!"
Die Wahrheit, Berlin, Germany

"She has a formidable musical intelligence. . ."
Penguin Guide to Jazz on CD

"Su Terry possesses a truly individual voice . . . she is especially compelling."
Cadence Magazine

"Superwoman of Jazz"
Hartford Courant

BY THE SAME AUTHOR

For The Curious

I Was a Jazz Musician for the FBI

Practice Like the Pros

Step One: Play Alto Sax

Step One: Play Tenor Sax

Step One: Play Clarinet

INDEX

Aaron, Jerome	56
AC/DC (group)	123
Albertson, Scot	178
Allegro	100
American Federation of Musicians	32
American Idol	6, 117
American Rifleman	151
Amos, Tori	8
Andrew Andrew (group)	66
Arbo, John	118
Architectural Digest	135, 144
Armstrong, Lance	99
Atwood, Margaret	32
Badenhausen, Otto A.	91
Barretto, Gil	9, 11, 15, 19, 30, 106, 136, 139, 163, 166, 170-172
Beatles, The (group)	123
Ben Hur, Roni	44
Bernstein, Felicia	90
Bernstein, Leonard	90-91
Bernstein, Shirley	90
Biden, Joe	17
bin Laden, Osama	41
Birdland	13, 169

Blakey, Art	61
Bland, Ed	54
Bloom, Jane Ira	27
Bloomberg, Michael	59
Blue Note, The	169
Blue Ribbon	66
Blues Rock Connection	22, 76
Bluestein, Joel	136
Boulanger, Nadia	55
Brin, Sergey	175
Brooklyn Lyceum	99
Brown, Paul	37
Bunker, Archie	95
Burns, Robert	90
Bush, George W.	85
Butterfly, Roxane	164
Caccavale, Eddie	37, 118
Camino Sur	44
Campbell, Wilbur	37
Caro, Marcia	90
Caravaggio	47
Carse, James	141
Carson, Johnny	9
Cassidy, David	58

Catingub, Matt	17
Charles, Nora	10
Cheng Man-Ching	141
Chicago (group)	7
Chopin, Frederick	122
Clinton, Bill	110
Clinton, George	125
Clinton, Hillary	12
Club Med	37
Club Venu	21
Coelho, Paulo	149
Cohan, George M.	82
Cole, Nat King	43
Coltrane, John	49, 57
Cook, Junior	79
Coon, Mike	65
Cooper, Sheila	83
Cranshaw, Bob	54
Crawford, Marc	79
Crefin, Elizabeth	7
Crow, Bill	100
Cunningham, Bob	44
Czak, Jim	49
Dalai Lama	67

Dantzler, Russ	59
Danza, Tony	117
Davis, Charles	44
Davis, Miles	47, 57, 71, 132
Dawson, Roger	87
de Chirico, Giorgio	71
de Maupassant, Guy	96
Deer Head Inn	53
Delta Airlines	32
Dennis, Donna	66
diCaprio, Leonardo	135
Dizzy's Club	169
Djilas, Milovan	148
Dunbar, Geoff	24
Durbal, Ramesh	144
Durgin, Lisa	56
Dvorak, Antonin	95
Eames, Charles & Ray	161
Einstein, Albert	45, 167
Elle Magazine	144
Ellington, Duke	60-61
Erickson, Milton	124
Feinstein's	52, 118
Ferlinghetti, Lawrence	133

Fierman, Marshall	30
Fitzgerald, Ed	180
Fitzgerald, Ella	95
Fortune Magazine	42
Fortune, Sonny	59
Foster, Jodie	16
Frank, Richard	22, 52, 76
Franklin, Ben	105
Friday Night Lights	14
Friedman, Janice	97
Friedman, Thomas L.	152
Gabor, Don	3
Gandalfe	126
Garfield, John	122
Getz, Stan	27, 95
Glasser, Dave	44
Glusac, Tom	44, 46
Goehring, Tom	53
Grammy Awards	112
Grey's Anatomy	6
Grice, Brian	65
Grimes, Henry	44
Gurdjieff, G.I.	67
Guy Lombardo Orchestra	97

Hadju, David	61
Hahn, Thich Nhat	149
Halpern, John	12
Ham, Larry	44
Hammer, Tardo	44
Hancock, Herbie	54
Hanks, Tom	103, 133
Hanser, Jonathan	109
Harper's Magazine	144
Harris, Barry	44, 46, 79
Hartt School, The	56
Hatfield, Ken	49
Hawkins, Coleman	44
Hayworth, Pat & Roger	5
Heffernan, Virginia	14
Hemingway, Ernest	149
Herold, Sandra	153
Hill, Jenny	43
Hill, Nelson	178
Holden, Stephen	52
Holder, Derwyn	42, 50
Holiday, Billie	27
Hull, Jeff	81
Isacoff, Stuart	175

Jackson, Chip	59
Jazzberry Jam (group)	21
Johann Sebastian Bach	18, 174
Johns, Steve	59
Jones, Elvin	59
Jones, Nat	44
Jordan, Clifford	37, 79
Juris, Vic	53
Kaiser Wilhelm	95
Kazan, Lainie	37
Keitel, Harvey	90
Khan, Genghis	25
Khan, Marty	124
King Kong	141
King, Nancy	45
King Louis XIV	95
King, Martin Luther Jr.	10
Kipling, Rudyard	66
Konikoff, Ross	59
Kraft, Pamela	136
Krause, Bernie	81
Kravitz, Lenny	38
Kripke, Eric	112
LaCroix, Lenny	118

la Rosa, Mark	47
Lake, Deb	44, 90, 134, 136
Lawson, Hugh	37
Leno, Jay	9
Letterman, Dave	110
Levant, Oscar	122
Leverett, Margot	34, 114
Liston, Melba	37
Liszt Academy	56
Liszt, Franz	122
Locke, Eddie	44
Longo, Mike	49
Mad Magazine	130
Madonna	122
Magritte, Rene	111
Manuszak, J.T.	35
Markoff, John	151
Marvin, Lee	19
Matthews, Chris	17
May, Earl	44
McCain, John	12, 120
McCarthy, Joseph	16
McKenna, Terence	136
McLean, Don	128

McLuhan, Marshall	75, 95
Mehegan, Gay	127
Mehegan, John	127
Menegio, Robert	103-104
Michelangelo	132
Mickey Sampson	24
Middleton, Andy	83
Miller, Deena	164
Minnelli, Liza	59
Mingus, Charles	95
Minton's	169
Mohegan Sun	117
Monk, Thelonious	55, 95
Moss, Bill	49
Mother Teresa	10
MTA	2, 178
Murrow, Edward R.	16
Nathanson, Roy	13
National Arts Club	78
New York Times	6, 14, 52, 75, 81, 85, 133, 143, 145, 148, 151, 152, 153, 175
New Yorker, The	93
Nicoll, Maurice	136
Nightingale, Florence	10

Nola Recording Studio	48
Obama, Barack	120
Olberman, Keith	18
Olympics	6
Open Center	141
Oracle, The	45
Ouspensky, P.D.	67
O'Connor, Flannery	161
Paar, Jack	9
Page, Larry	175
Palin, Sarah	17
Parent Magazine	144
Parker, Charlie	11, 81, 123
Paul, Ron	120
Payne, Cecil	167-168
PBS	15
Pegu Club	66
Perla, Gene	53
Persip, Charli	126
Ponamarev, Valery	32
Pori Festival	59
Post, Johnny	49
Price, Tim	46, 79, 167
Princess Diana	113

Profitlich, Markus	84
Queen Elizabeth	60
Rafferty, Adam	49
Ram Dass	133
Raoul's	140
Rascal Flatts (group)	58
Rasputin	95
Reed, Rex	52
Reese, Andrea	113
Reeves, Dianne	17
Reeves, Keanu	135
Rembrandt	75
Ries, Tim	126
Rodin	141
Rolling Stones, The (group)	123, 126
Rossy, Yves	176
Rubin, Saul	82
Rubin, Vanessa	46
Ruckert, Ann	52
Sand, George	122, 161
Schumann Resonance	72
Schwarzenegger, Arnold	135
Scott, Cynthia	46
Scott, Shirley	54

Seeger, Pete	55
Seuss, Dr.	28
Shakespeare, William	43
Shoup, Dave	118
Silverstein, Michael J.	144
Simon, Paul	109
Smith, Winston	176
Solon, Gene	124
Solzhenitsyn, Alexander	148
Sotheby's	70
Spaulding, James	54
Stalin, Joseph	148
Stephans, Michael	53
Stewart, Jimmy	19
Stravinsky, Igor	55
Strayhorn, Billy	60-61
Sunshine, Elysa	106, 163
Surgeon General	148
Sweet Rhythm	168
Szabo, Rich	5
Tanzbrunnen Theatre	84
Tatarsky, Elias & Nellie	24
Tate, Grady	54
Tatum, Art	60

Tavern on the Green	78
Taylor, Dr. Billy	59
Terry, Alfred	24
Terry, Annamaria	4
Terry, Brian	35, 136, 140, 158
Terry, Clark	24
Terry, Ellen	24
Terry, Herbert	24
Terry, Jessica	69
Tester, Jon	78
Tower of Power (group)	59
Town Hall	146
Truss, Lynne	30
TSA	31
Utne Reader	151
Valenti, Gianni	13
Vaughan, Sarah	17, 71, 95
Venus of Willendorf	146
Vick, Harold	53-54
Village Vanguard	168
Vivaldi, Antonio	51
Vogue	144
Wagner, Richard	95
Watson, Dr.	102

Waugh, Evelyn	161
Webster, Ben	17
Weekly Reader	151
Wendholt, Scott	59
Williams, Leroy	44
Winfrey, Oprah	110
Wired Magazine	151
Wojcicki, Anne	175
Woods, Phil	8
Wyands, Richard	44
Yamaha	8
Yudkin, Dave	56
Zawadi, Kiane	44
Zhang San Feng	71, 107

READER DISCUSSION GUIDE
FOR
INSIDE THE MIND OF A MUSICIAN

• In the author's preface, the reader is welcomed 'inside the mind of a musician.' Do you think the ability to communicate in a wordless language like music would give one a different perspective on life?

• The ancient Troubadours entertained the courts of medieval Europe; when they weren't entertaining, their opinions were sought out during political discourse. Do you think it's appropriate, in today's world, for musicians to try to influence public opinion on political matters?

• Mike Coon says "musicians are creatures of the absurd." How would you interpret that statement?

• If you know Brooklyn, can you comment on why you think it's a place that nurtures artists and artistic creativity?

• After reading this book, do you feel you have indeed been 'inside the mind of a musician'? Would you say the author is a 'typical' musician, or not?

• Discuss any insights you've gleaned from reading this book, on the subjects of:
    Music
    The Music Business
    Politics
    Society
    Philosophy
    Brooklyn